D0722301

Andrew Marvell

Andrew Marvell, artist unknown, 1655–60.

Andrew Marvell: His Life and Writings

John Dixon Hunt

Cornell University Press

Ithaca, New York

For

Arnold and Bess Stein

and

Charles and Eula Singleton:

Nor less the Rooms within commends
Daily new *Furniture* of *Friends*

First published 1978 by Cornell University Press.

International Standard Book Number 0–8014–1202–1
Library of Congress Catalog Number 78–57689

Printed in Great Britain by
Unwin Brothers Limited
The Gresham Press
Old Woking, Surrey

Contents

List of Plates

6

7

The device used throughout is taken from Marvell's stag seal (The Bodleian Library: MS Rawl. Letters 50, fol. 130v); it was first reproduced by John Wallace in *Destiny His Choice* (Cambridge University Press, 1968).

Preface

Andrew Marvell's poetry is richly, densely packed with meaning. By contrast, his life is rather barren of absorbing detail. Writing the Marvell volume for the English Men of Letters series in 1905, Augustine Birrell remarked that 'A more elusive, non-recorded character is hardly to be found'. It may seem, then, rather foolhardy to attempt the poet's biography. Two reasons, however, have suggested themselves for undertaking it.

First, there have been since Birrell many discoveries of small biographical facts, even of apparently trivial local details of Marvell's career; the files of *Notes and Queries* and the correspondence columns of the *Times Literary Supplement* are scattered with contributions towards a larger portrait. So that it seemed worthwhile in 1978 (the tercentenary of his death) to gather some of these scattered materials and try and shape them into a fuller picture.

Second, my experience of teaching Marvell's poetry has led me to believe that giving a context to the handful of brilliant lyrics upon which attention usually focuses can enhance them. Such a context requires extending our reading to other, less famous poems, to his letters and to his prose satires, and these in their turn lead into his political career. I suspect that for the academic and non-academic reader alike of Marvell's poetry it is rather bewildering to think that the author of 'To his Coy Mistress' also wrote 'The Last Instructions to a Painter'. Some attempt to read them in the larger patterns of Marvell's writing and life may illuminate both as well as lead us to a more exciting and informed view of a man 'scarse fully paralleled by any'.

When the Victorian critic, John Ruskin, first came across Marvell's poems, he wrote to tell his father (who recorded the remarks in his diary) that he found that it was 'the poetry of a strong man toiling and fighting through troublous life'*. Now, the Victorians were much devoted to 'life and works' studies, so Ruskin's testimony is not particularly objective and, in addition, may well betray his own experience of writing and living. But Ruskin's impromptu reaction upon first reading Marvell still seems to me the right instinct: namely, to relate, as best we can, Marvell's poetry to his experience of life in seventeenth-century Europe. There are times —notably the all-important 1640s—for which we still do not have anything like adequate material for a proper biography of Marvell. I have there been able only to suggest possible itineraries and interests for his European travels, sketching mainly a map of the garden sights which, in the light of later poems, may have attracted his attention at that time.

---

*Bembridge MS 33, p.30 (entry for June 1852), quoted by permission of the Ruskin Galleries, Bembridge School, Isle of Wight.

The illustrations in this volume serve basically two functions: to image the people and places in Marvell's life; and to provide a visual anthology of the cultural artifacts of the seventeenth century—portraits, historical and topographical paintings, miniatures, medals, books and their illustrations or even annotations, prints, music—so that the reader may derive for himself some composite diagram of the times in which Andrew Marvell lived.

I have depended heavily on the work of many Marvellians, whose scholarship and criticism are acknowledged in my notes. Special mention must be made here of H.M. Margoliouth's indispensable edition of *The Poems and Letters*, revised by two other exemplary Marvellians, Pierre Legouis and Elsie Duncan-Jones. I have found their commentary and notes (together with those in the more convenient Penguin edition of *The Complete Poems* by E.S. Donno) of constant service.

Final drafts of this work have been scrutinized by a variety of readers, to whose patience and larger knowledge I am much indebted. Foremost among them is Mrs Duncan-Jones, who gave of her time and Marvellian expertise to a complete stranger, thereby preventing his mistakes and generally helping to sharpen his arguments. Michael Cordner and Dinos Patrides, former colleagues at the University of York, demonstrated the continuing services of friendship by apt mixtures of encouragement and scepticism, while Warren Chernaik and Alun Davies at the University of London initiated new contacts with their comments. Arnold Stein took time from his own writing on a sabbatical in London to prune the typescript of its more vulgar errors.

For help with obtaining photographs I am much indebted to Miss Joan Dawson (for kindly allowing me to visit Nun Appleton), Miss E.A. Evans at the National Portrait Gallery, Mr R.T. Tolson, Headmaster of Hull Grammar School, Lesley Dunn and Ann Crowther at the Hull Museums, Professor Douglas Chambers, Mr Michael Youngblood and Mr David Whiteley.

1 A Gentleman whose name is
Mr Marvile

The difficulties facing a biographer of Andrew Marvell were epitomized by his eighteenth-century editor, Captain Thompson, R.N.—'He had no wife and his gallantries are not known'[1]. For all the detailed, even ingenious, exegesis of his poetry by twentieth-century critics, Marvell remains mysteriously hidden from us today behind much playful, artful refusal to commit himself to anything that would help in bringing a picture of an obviously complex character into some focus. The literary critic can offer little assistance, for the poems—quite properly—yield few biographical facts. His coy mistress does not illuminate his life or anything about him except his literary self-consciousness. The paucity of hard biographical data simply accentuates the enigmas that presented themselves to his contemporaries as they do to us today.

John Aubrey records that 'He was in his conversation very modest, and of very few words; and though he loved wine he would never drinke hard in company'[2]. The comment identifies a cagey, taciturn man, something of a solitary, at least a private, person. Yet his adversary in a pamphlet war of the 1670s, Samuel Parker (see below, pp.166 ff.), said that he had the tongue of a bargee. Perhaps a controversialist inevitably arouses very animated disagreements; but I suspect Marvell's own ambiguities of character, his own taste for disputation, debate, and even disguise, coloured others' assessment of him. Certainly, there were various, often conflicting, judgements. Milton wrote of 'his singular desert for the State to make use of'; yet Marvell could be quarrelsome and physically violent in the House of Commons. Dryden said he 'was the first Presbyterian Scribler who sanctify'd Libels and Scurrility to the use of the Good Old Cause'. On the other hand, Rochester praised him for exposing folly. During the Restoration years he was variously hailed as a coffee-house wit, a hack writer paid for by dissenters, a stooge of Milton's (impotent and homosexual, to boot), and an affected *Ingenioso*.

Something of this perplexing kaleidoscope of judgements is mirrored in the portraits that have at various times been considered to be painted from Marvell himself[3]. Now portraiture—visual images of a personality—must capture in a fixed and timeless pose all the variety of a subject. It is a difficulty that confronts any discussion of the portraits of Andrew

Marvell, and by extension any biographical portrait of him. It is also a problem with which Marvell himself wittily plays in his poem, 'The Gallery' [pp.31–2]*. To illustrate a person adequately we need, as Alexander Pope realized in the eighteenth century, when he wrote about female portraiture, a whole series of images: 'How many pictures of one Nymph we view,/All how unlike each other, all how true!'⁴. Pope's sense of human variety and unpredictability owes much to Montaigne's delighted observation of our inconstancies; for the moralist and portraitist such instability is particularly perplexing, as Pope saw:

> Arcadia's Countess, here, in ermined pride,
> Is, there, Pastora by a fountain side.
> Here Fannia, leering on her own good man,
> And there, a naked Leda with a Swan.
> Let then the Fair one beautifully cry,
> In Magdalen's loose hair and lifted eye,
> Or dressed in smiles of sweet Cecilia shine,
> With simpering Angels, Palms, and Harps divine...

Pope's lady, as Marvell said of Clora in 'The Gallery', has 'grown a num'rous Colony'.

In Marvell's gallery of portraits Clora is seen successively as 'Inhumane Murtheress', 'Aurora', and 'an Enchantress' in a cave, or '*Venus* in her pearly boat'. But a complication of this poem is that the poet has adopted the conventional device of representing the soul as a beautiful woman (think of images of Psyche); the portraits, then, are innumerable *self*-portraits—

> *Clora* come view my Soul, and tell
> Whether I have contriv'd it well.
> Now all its several lodgings lye
> Compos'd into one Gallery;
> And the great *Arras*-hangings, made
> Of various Faces, by are laid:
> That, for all Furniture, you'l find
> Only your Picture in my Mind.

It is entirely characteristic of Marvell, as he emerges in his own writings and in the fragmentary incidents recorded of his life, that he signals himself by such a multiplicity of self-portraits: 'These Pictures and a thousand more... my Gallery do store'. Yet it is further typical that his amusing repertoire of self-portraits is, after all, only a series of images of Clora herself.

We must bear in mind, then, 'all the Forms' of Marvell's soul as we trace

---

*See p.191 for explanation of references.

1 (left) Andrew Marvell, engraved portrait from *Miscellaneous Poems*, 1681.
2 (right) Andrew Marvell, engraved portrait by James Basire from *Works*, 1776.

his career as poet, tutor, traveller, civil servant and politician. As the first of these, he was much drawn to poems where he could be attentive to tensions and contraries or where he could even present them in dialogues or debates between (say) the 'Resolved Soul' and 'Created Pleasure'. In a piece like 'The Nymph complaining for the death of her Faun' [pp.23–6] the poet puts himself into another (very different) person's psychological agitation and dramatizes its extreme, touching and intense contraries. As politician, he seems to have practised what John Wallace has called a 'scrupulous timeserving', offering his allegiance to the 'providential constitution' of succeeding regimes[5]. And in that fine moment of political poetry, 'An Horatian Ode upon Cromwel's Return from Ireland' [pp.91–4], Marvell characteristically contrives some appreciation of Charles I's conduct on the scaffold as well as some shrewd analysis of Cromwell's 'forced Pow'r' all within a piece that is still largely commendation of the parliamentary soldier.

In the gallery of Marvell portraits only one is certainly authentic: this is the 'Nettleton' version in the National Portrait Gallery (frontispiece), so

3 (left) *Andrew Marvell*, artist unknown, 1662.

4 (right) *Young man* (once known as 'Andrew Marvell'), miniature by F.S. Smiadecki.

named because of its donor, a great nephew of the poet. It pictures closely enough the man whom Aubrey describes as 'of middling stature, pretty strong sett, roundish faced, cherry cheek't, hazell eie, browne haire'. The costume dates it 1655–60, so that Marvell would be in his mid or late thirties; he was then either abroad as a tutor to Cromwell's ward and intended son-in-law or assistant to Milton as Latin Secretary. In either capacity Marvell would be more in the public eye than heretofore, and the pose of the 'Nettleton' portrait conveys this status. There is self-conscious stylishness about the full, dark brown hair and the tassels to his plain white bands. If the nose, lips and chin strike us as somewhat tough, at least forthright, the eyes, though sombre, suggest vivacity, subtlety and curiosity. This image is modified in the engraved portrait, published posthumously in the *Miscellaneous Poems* of 1681 (plate 1); this perhaps derives from the 'Nettleton' portrait (the reversal strongly supports this), for the tassels and the determined features are roughly the same, while he sports a fashionable full-bottomed wig, for which he was often mocked[6]. But a cloak has now been added, in which the poet seems to wrap himself

5 (left) *Young man* (once identified as Marvell), by Adriaen Hanneman, 1658.

6 (right) *Portrait of a Man* (known as 'Andrew Marvell'), by Van der Helst.

away; the eyes still stare and, less reposeful, are set in a face made to appear more worn by the texture of the engraving. It could be that this published image in the *Miscellaneous Poems* is derived jointly from the 'Nettleton' and from another, known as the 'Hollis', portrait. This latter is named after its eighteenth-century owner, Thomas Hollis, a republican, traveller and dilettante. We know that it was engraved in 1760 by Cipriani and again by Basire in 1776, this second engraving being published in the edition of Marvell's *Works* of that year (plate 2). The 'Hollis' portrait, or more likely a copy of it, belongs to the Wilberforce Museum, Hull (plate 3). The inscription records its subject's age as forty-one. It has a strong claim to be Marvell: the coarser texture of the face is closer to the sombre air of the 1681 engraving than to the more delicate complexion of the 'Nettleton', the hair is less distinct and crisp, the bands much more austere and stiff. Thomas Hollis is supposed to have contrasted his portrait with the livelier and wittier image we 'might expect' of Marvell and to have attributed it to the coarser, uncongenial effects of the Restoration[7].

Two portraits, now lost, that we would dearly love to have are those by

Peter Lely, one of the accomplished portraitists of the mid-seventeenth century (this is recorded by the antiquary, George Vertue) and by Samuel Cooper, the portraitist of Oliver Cromwell and Charles II among others (see plate 62)[8]. As it is, we have only a variety of exhibits, where the attribution to Marvell depends rather upon wishful thinking than scholarship. As Samuel Redgrove wrote in 1866 in his introduction to the *Catalogue of the First Special Exhibition of National Portraits* at the South Kensington Museum, when two 'Marvell' items were on display—numbers 804 and 861—'Old portraits are now vamped up, and christened with great names; spurious copies are manufactured, and passed off as originals...'

Three items in particular, which have at some point in time been christened with the great name of Marvell, are worth considering, simply because the urge to associate them with his name tells us something about the various images of the poet and parliamentarian that have imposed themselves upon the public fancy. The first is a miniature (plate 4) and shows a young man, perhaps not yet out of his teens. The second, by Adriaen Hanneman, reveals a slightly older and rather mannered man (plate 5). We could certainly do with both for our 'several lodgings' of Marvell's gallery, for their 'invented forms' consort well with images of the poet we derive from his poems. A third, by Van der Helst, shows a man with some resemblance to those of the 'Nettleton' and 'Hollis' portraits (plate 6).

It would have been most unusual for a person of Marvell's status to have had a miniature done of himself in his late teens—by the time Cooper would have done the one already noted Marvell's position might have warranted it. Yet the youth in plate 4 is plausible enough, since the features accord with those of the 'Nettleton' version; furthermore, the elegant lace collar, the slightly raised right eyebrow and the dimple that gives the rather feminine mouth a quizzical turn could certainly figure for both the undergraduate author of 'Ad Regem Carolum Parodia' [p.1], verses published in 1637 to honour the birth of Charles I's daughter, Anne, and the brief convert to Roman Catholicism two years later (see below, pp.21–4). There is, finally, something in this miniature of that deportment for which Richard Lovelace, the Cavalier lyricist, was noted in 1634—'the most amiable and beautiful person that ever eye beheld, a person also of innate modesty, virtue and courtly deportment' [I.239]. We assume that Lovelace and Marvell met in Cambridge in the later 1630s; perhaps the miniature, eloquent both of modesty and of courtliness, could be Marvell's trying of the device of lyricist in the Lovelace mould. Yet over a decade later, when Marvell contributed a commendatory poem to Lovelace's *Lucasta*, published in 1649 one month before the King's execution, he noted the changed times:

16

A Gentleman whose name is Mr Marvile

Sir,
    Our times are much degenerate from those
Which your sweet Muse which your fair Fortune chose,
And as complexions alter with the Climes,
Our wits have drawne th'infection of our times.
That candid Age no other way could tell
To be ingenious, but by speaking well.
Who best could prayse, had then the greatest prayse,
Twas more esteemd to give, then weare the Bayes:
Modest ambition studi'd only then,
To honour not her selfe, but worthy men.
These vertues now are banisht out of Towne,
Our Civill Wars have lost the Civicke crowne.
He highest builds, who with most Art destroys,
And against others Fame his owne employs.   [pp.2–3]

The mannerist pose of the young man in plate 5 suggests the mocking assumption of lovers' roles that in later, infected, times was Marvell's only poetic resource. 'The unfortunate Lover' [pp.29–31] and 'The Fair Singer' [p.33], for example, are the melodramatic postures of a poet playing with conventional and romantic language. The former talks of 'This masque of quarrelling Elements', an apt theatrical metaphor for the man portrayed by Hanneman. The mock logic and self-regarding eroticism of the second might also be appropriate speech for that elegant, rather deliberately 'melancholic' figure. The right hand, so posed against the breast, declares an ironic nostalgia for the 'world enough and time' which allowed former lovers the luxury of idle pursuit and coy dalliance. Still, this portrait, signed and dated 1658 by Hanneman, is unlikely to be of Marvell, however much its image and the fine quality of its painting tempt us. Hanneman had been in The Hague since 1640 and no visit of Marvell's is recorded for 1658; some of his letters to the British Resident at The Hague [II.307–8] leave little doubt that he was engaged in London at the time. This allows only a visit to Holland about 1656, when he was accompanying William Dutton to Saumur in France (see below, p.132) and when he might have sat to Hanneman.

The third portrait (plate 6) is identified as Marvell at the Wilberforce Museum in Hull. Facial resemblances to the 'Hollis' version in the same room are somewhat tempting, and the impression conveyed of steady vision and slightly sardonic, even aggressive, manner might fit the Restoration satirist (below, chapters 8 and 9). The identification of the sitter as Marvell at least reminds us that his reputation for a very long time after his death was as a patriot—satirist and parliamentary man—and not the poet which the attributions of plates 4 and 5 celebrate.

Portraits are improvised icons, the outward shows of what Marvell called an 'active Minde' [I.5] and can only hint at an essential variousness.

We treat of difficult matters when we seek to elucidate any substantial personality from them, and we should recall the (maybe sceptical) title of one of Marvell's own Latin poems on another such occasion—'To a Gentleman that only upon the sight of the Author's writing, had given a Character of his Person and Judgement of his Fortune'. We must pass beyond such trials to that richer, yet altogether more difficult, region that Wallace Stevens celebrates in 'An Ordinary Evening in New Haven':

> A blank underlies the trials of device,
> The dominant blank, the unapproachable.

2 By the Tide of Humber

At Winestead-in-Holderness, in Yorkshire, where his father was the rector, Andrew Marvell was born on 31 March 1621, 'being Easter-even'; he was baptized on 5 April. He was the first son, there being already three daughters in the family, and there was to be one other son who died in infancy.

It was some time not later than 1608/9 that the poet's father, also called Andrew, had moved north to Yorkshire, becoming curate at Flamborough. A few years later, on 22 October 1612, he married Anne Pease, a Yorkshire woman. Two years later still, when Andrew senior obtained his first living, they moved to Holderness, south-east of Hull along the spur of land that dwindles eventually into Spurn Head, bent southwards across Humbermouth. The entry in the church-book, transcribed by Grosart, Marvell's nineteenth-century editor, read:

Andrew Marvell, parson of Winestead, was inducted into the corporall and peacable possession of the sayd parsonage by Mr Marmaduke Brooke, deane, parson of Rosse, upon Easter even, being George's day, the twenty-third of Aprill, and in the yeare of our Lord 1614. [I.xx–xxi]

The Marvells were originally Cambridgeshire folk, for their name can be traced back at least to 1279 in the area of Meldreth; Pierre Legouis reports that a house called 'The Marvells' was still known there in the nineteenth century[9]. Andrew Marvell senior had gone up to the recently founded

18

Emmanuel College, Cambridge, becoming bachelor of arts in 1605 and master of arts in 1608. Since 1584 Emmanuel had quickly established itself as a Puritan stronghold, and it was doubtless the father's education there that made him what Anthony à Wood reports, 'Facetious and yet calvinistic'[10]. His son was to write to him that he had been 'a Conformist to the established Rites of the Church of *England*, though I confess none of the most over-running or eager in them' [*RT*.203-4]. He lived, his son also affirmed, 'with some measure of reputation, both for Piety and Learning'. To those qualities, inner convictions and pursuits rather than the outward 'rites' of conformity, Marvell, father and son, not surprisingly attended. Had he survived into the Civil War years the father would presumably have supported the Long Parliament; for we assume that resistance to oppression was a family strain, since a yeoman called Andrew Marvell, probably the poet's grandfather, left Cambridgeshire rather than pay two pounds of a forced loan, levied by Charles I without parliamentary sanction.

Of the father's career in Hull, to which he moved in 1624 as 'Lecturer' in Holy Trinity Church and Master of the Charterhouse, we have various testimony. There is the biased attack of his son's enemy, Parker, who affirmed that in the 'late Rebellion...none were more conspicuous for loyalty than the Dignified Clergy, and none greater Incendiaries than the Mercenary Preachers and Lecturers, who subsisted purely by the Benevolence and arbitrary Pensions of the People'[11]. The burgesses of Hull had chosen the Reverend Andrew Marvell as their preacher, which explains Parker's rather snide emphasis; yet it is presumably their appreciation that Thomas Fuller records in his *Worthies of England* (1662), where we learn that he 'was well beloved' in Hull:

Most *facetious* in his discourse, yet *grave* in his *carriage*, a most excellent preacher, who like a good husband never *broached* what he had new brewed, but preached what he had pre-studied some time before. Insomuch that he was wont to say that he would crosse the common proverb, which called *Saturday* the working day and *Monday* the holy day of preachers.

At least in the nineteenth century many manuscript sermons and addresses by Marvell senior survived and were seen by Alexander Grosart, who was impressed by the preacher's 'fearlessly outspoken character', his wide reading in classics and the church fathers and his 'tireless activity' [I.xxv].

The move from Winestead-in-Holderness to Hull meant that the family occupied a house surrounded by gardens just to the north of the city walls and near the banks of the River Hull (see plate 7). This dwelling was provided for the Master of the Charterhouse, an almshouse founded in 1384, of which we gather that Marvell's father proved a capable administrator. Otherwise, the move ensured that the son was

19

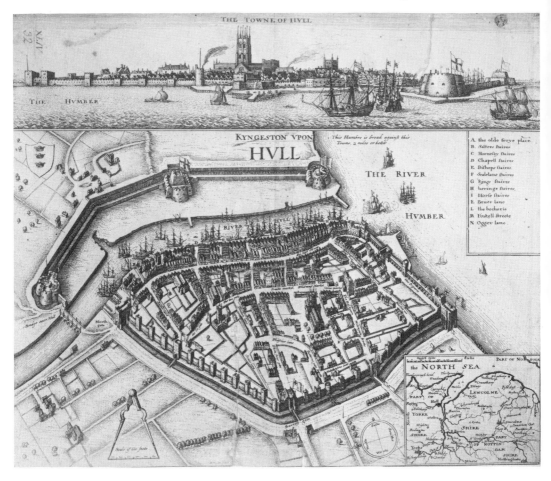

7 Kingston upon Hull, engraved plan by Wenceslas Hollar, 1640s.

'well-educated in grammar learning'[12]—that is to say at the Grammar
School, near Holy Trinity. Andrew Marvell himself recorded his
impressions of the fairly traditional curriculum: 'For as I remember this
scanning was a liberal art that we learn'd at Grammar School, and to scan
verses as he does the Author's prose before we did or were obliged to
understand them'[13]. Doubtless Marvell also got some alternative
'education', as Parker was to complain, 'among Boat-Swains and
Cabin-boys, whose Phrases...you learn't in your childhood'. But after 14
December 1633, when Andrew matriculated at Trinity College,
Cambridge, he was among an altogether different crew.

3 Musa Cantabrigiensis

The college to which Marvell's father (presumably) chose to send him was fairly moderate in its churchmanship, somewhere between the Puritan Emmanuel and the ritualist Peterhouse. The University was a miniature version of the religious disputes at large in the country, and it is worth our while to linger over such matters not only as perhaps an early context for Marvell's Latitudinarian pleas for tolerance in his later pamphlets (see below, chapter 9), but as a means of explaining in some measure the strange circumstance of Marvell's brief conversion by the Jesuits while an undergraduate.

The Puritanism and Calvinism that his father would have known at college had begun their emigration by the 1630s to the new Cambridge, in Massachusetts; by 1633 George Herbert wrote that 'Religion stands on tiptoe in our land/Ready to pass to the American strand'. And Harvard College was named in 1639 after the master of Emmanuel, recently arrived and deceased there. The Protestant traditions which dominated the younger Marvell's years at Cambridge in the 1630s were essentially those surviving from Elizabethan days; the University proved more stubborn than Oxford in resisting the reforms proposed by Laud, the Chancellor at Oxford and, from 1633, the year of Marvell's matriculation, Archbishop of Canterbury. This resistance derived much of its strength from the presence in Cambridge of such as Benjamin Whichcote, elected in 1636 as lecturer in Trinity Church by the citizens, as Marvell's father had been in Hull. This founder of the Cambridge Platonists was re-energizing the old Puritan spirit, giving it an impetus towards toleration and towards the reconciliation of reason and mysticism. Marvell would have imbibed more of such Platonism from a preacher in his own college chapel, John Sherman, some of whose sermons were gathered into a delightful book which is, in its author's own words, 'learned, I say, and eloquent'[14].

But other factions were at work. Fuller's *History of Cambridge University* (1655) tells of the 'general complaint of most moderate men that many in the University, both in the schools and pulpits, approached the opinions of the Church of Rome nearer than ever before' (p.166). And he notes, apropos of the spate of building activity at this period, that college chapels were 'graced with the accession of organs. And seeing musick is one of the

8 Peterhouse Chapel, engraving from D. Loggan's *Cantabrigia Illustrata*, 1690.

liberal arts, how could it be quarrelled at in an University if they sang with understanding both of the matter and manner thereof. Yet some took great distaste thereat as attendancie to superstition' (p.167). Into such ritualist *cénacles* the Jesuits could presumably insinuate themselves with ease. At Peterhouse, which we know to have been a base for Romanist agents, the new chapel (consecrated 1632) may have epitomized some of these 'superstitions' with its evocation of a Catholic heritage in the perpendicular tracery, windows and turrets, remarkably blended with ogee niches, classical motifs and the fantastical curl of its gables (plate 8)[15]. One of the Fellows elected at Peterhouse in 1635 was Richard Crashaw, who had converted to Roman Catholicism by the mid 1640s. Meanwhile he interested himself in liturgical music, memories of which may have lingered when Marvell came to compose 'Musicks Empire' [pp.50–1]:

> Then Musick, the Mosaique of the Air,
> Did of all these a solemn noise prepare:
> With which She gain'd the Empire of the Ear,
> Including all between the Earth and Sphear.

Crashaw's other involvement was with the community at Little Gidding founded by Nicolas Ferrar, who left his merchant's business to establish a devout family enclave, dedicated to religious observance and work (they made book-binding their particular occupation); among others, Charles I sought a brief solace there in 1642. Since Marvell and Crashaw published poems together in 1637 it may be that they shared some discussions upon retirement. It was, at any rate, a theme of much concern to Marvell in later years and one to which there was much philosophical and practical attention paid (as at Little Gidding, Great Tew, or Nun Appleton) during the middle years of the century.

Marvell's connections with Peterhouse and its members we may infer from a curious document found among the Marvell papers at Hull in the nineteenth century. It is a letter to the Reverend Marvell from an unknown correspondent, who wrote because he had heard that a similar 'prank' as befell his son had been 'used towards y[r] sonne':

Worthy S[r]—Mr Breercliffe being with me to-day, I related unto him a fearfull passage lately at Cambridg touching a sonne of mine, Bachelor of Arts in Katharine Hall, wch was this. He was lately invited to a supper in towne by a gentlewoman, where was one Mr Nichols a felow of Peterhouse, and another or two masters of arts, I know not directly whether felowes or not: my sonne having noe p'ferment, but living meerly of my penny, they pressed him much to come to live at their house, and for chamber and extraordinary bookes they promised farre: and then earnestly moved him to goe to Somerset house, where they could doe much for p'ferring him to some eminent place, and in conclusion to popish arguments to seduce him soe rotten and unsavory as being overheard it was brought in question before the heads of the University: Dr *Cosens* being Vice Chancelor noe punishment is injoined him: but on Ash-wednesday next a recantation in regent house of some popish tenets Nicols let fall: I p'ceive by Mr Breercliffe some such prank used towards y^r sonne: I desire to know what ye did therin... [Grosart, I.xxviii]

There is a family tradition that Andrew Marvell, converted to Roman Catholicism, probably in 1639, fled from the university town and was tracked by his father to London, discovered—'characteristically', as every biographer is forced to say—at a bookseller's and returned to his college.

Received back into the moderate world of Trinity, Marvell became Bachelor of Arts and presumably stayed in residence (he had been elected scholar of his college in 1638) with a view to proceeding to his Master's degree. His studies, of which he himself tells us virtually nothing, would continue to be based primarily in logic and rhetoric, where he would have been trained in the skills of disputation: Marvell, later in his career, wrote of such discipline that it taught one 'how to erect a *Thesis*, defend it *Pro* or *Con* with a serviceable distinction' [*RT*.29]. In addition he would have been instructed in Aristotle's *Ethics, Politics* and *Physics* and, depending upon his individual tutor, a range of classical literature and history. If a recent, exciting suggestion by Elsie Duncan-Jones is correct, Marvell distinguished himself in these curricula sufficiently to get himself represented in a play by a fellow student. She suggests that the Latin play by Abraham Cowley, *Naufragium Joculare,* written to be performed at Trinity in 1638, contains a part which Marvell may have played—or, at least, a part in which he may have been glanced at. This is the tutor, Gnomicus, repeatedly referred to as *vir admirabilis,* the marvellous man (the pun through translation would be par for Trinity undergraduates); he sets up a market in Latin jokes and promises to provide the recipes for persuasion, mockery and panegyric—then, says Gnomicus/Marvell, 'everbody will marvel at you as they do at me'[16].

But we do not need this glimpse, however tempting its plausibility makes it, into Marvell's student accomplishments. Even a casual leafing through the notes to modern editions of his work will reveal how wide a range of classical reading he must have acquired; the poems and pamphlets themselves testify to his skills in Gnomicus' line. Since the Master of Trinity was the learned Thomas Comber, who 'excelled in the Hebrew, Arabic, Coptic, Samaritan, Syriac, Chaldee, Persian, Greek, and Latin languages, and also in French, Spanish, and Italian, which he not only understood but spoke'[17], it is probable that Marvell at least initiated the study of languages with which Milton credited him in the 1650s; it is, of course, inconceivable that he would not have maintained and extended his studies after University.

We *do* know that he had begun to write verses, for two pieces—in Greek and Latin—appeared in Συνωδία , a traditional tribute that the birth of

Princess Anne elicited from a dutiful University (Oxford also obliged with its volume). The Cambridge poets, publishing under the title of *Musa Cantabrigiensis*, included, besides Marvell, Crashaw, Cowley and that Edward King whose death later in the year was mourned in Milton's *Lycidas*. The sixteen-year-old scholar, Marvell, imitates Horace's ode to Octavius after Actium, substituting the recent Cambridge plague for the portents after Caesar's death: Charles and his queen will, however, repeople and restore the depleted country. Within twelve years, as it happened, Charles was executed; but the verses were only a literary exercise.

The plague had been raging, too, in Hull and the Reverend Marvell was much praised for the succour he brought to its citizens. Two of his daughters had meanwhile married into well-to-do local families, the Blaydes and the Popples. In 1638 Mrs Marvell died, but by the end of that same year the father had remarried, a widow by the name of Lucy Alured. However, he was not to enjoy this second marriage for long: in January 1640 he was drowned while crossing the Humber in the company (tradition has it) of a 'Mrs Skinner' and a young couple on their way to be married. Their deaths (and disappearance of the bodies) became much embroidered in local folklore during the eighteenth and nineteenth centuries, but its superstitions and romanticisms have no foundation. We cannot even be sure who the father's companion was on the fatal crossing, while the tradition that a *Miss* Skinner drowned and that her mother befriended the nineteen-year-old Andrew and paid for him to travel seems equally unfounded[18].

4 Foure Years Abroad

But travel he did. For this we have the testimony of John Milton in the letter, already quoted, of 1652/3—'he hath spent foure years abroad in Holland, France, Italy, and Spaine, to very good purpose...and the gaining of those four languages'. Since he was back home at the very latest by 1649, perhaps by 1645, Marvell may have left England in 1641 or 1642, the year of the outbreak of Civil War.

Much remains hidden to us of these crucial years. We *know* that he left

Cambridge around 1641, for the Conclusion-book at Trinity records that Marvell, among others, 'in regard tht some of them are reported to be maryed and tht others looke not after their dayes nor Acts. . . shall be out of their places unless thei shew just cause to the Coll for the contrary in 3 months' [Grosart, I.xxxiii]. Perhaps he absented himself too much after his father's death; he did not join Crashaw, Cowley and others in a further loyal collection of verses for the birth of the future Duke of Gloucester in 1640, so that he may even have left by then. The country had elected members of the Short Parliament and again of the Long Parliament in 1640: on both occasions Cambridge chose Oliver Cromwell, but whether Marvell was in the city we do not know. Legouis reports a 'local tradition' that he served his 'clerkship' at Hull and offers a 'reasonable guess' that he had entered the trading-house of one of his brothers-in-law soon after his father's death[19].

Also uncertain is whether he fought in the Civil War. Whatever dates he was abroad would certainly entail his having missed some of the fighting. Furthermore, we have his famous (infamous, for his contemporaries, or, at best, mysterious) remark in *The Rehearsal Transpros'd* of 1672 that 'the cause was too good to have been fought for'; this at least may be taken to imply that the writer himself did not engage in the combat. The context of the remark also corroborates this implication: Archbishop Laud

moreover had a mind to try the same dangerous Experiment in *Scotland*, and sent thither the Book of the *English Liturgy*, to be imposed upon them. What followed thereupon, is yet within the compass of most Mens memories. And how War broke out, and then to be sure Hell's broke loose. Whether it were a War of Religion, or of Liberty, is not worth the labour to enquire. Which-soever was at the top, the other was at the bottom; but upon considering all, I think the Cause was too good to have been fought for. Men ought to have trusted God; they ought and might have trusted the King with that whole matter. The *Arms of the Church are Prayers and Tears*, the Arms of the Subjects are Patience and Petitions. The King himself being of so accurate and piercing a judgement, would soon have felt where it stuck. For men may spare their pains where Nature is at work, and the world will not go the faster for our driving. Even as his present Majesties happy Restoration did it self, so all things else happen in their best and proper time, without any need of our officiousness. [*RT*.134–5]

Marvell's confidence in a providential outcome, which men's wise tolerance must assist, separates him from his friend, John Milton; but Milton also expressed himself forcibly on his absence from the battlefields and in a work that Marvell was to praise, when he 'exchanged the toils of war, in which any stout trooper may outdo me, for those labours which I better understood'[20]. This conviction that no system was bad enough to destroy a good man or good enough to save a bad one may have come to Marvell later, after the various 'systems' between Charles I's and his son's had all been tested; yet even such a delayed determination to avoid 'officiousness' must have taken root earlier, whether by the chances or calculations of travelling abroad.

It was, we learn from a contemporary book[21] one of the aims of travel that it 'setleth his affections more sure to his owne Country'. Even if Marvell's patriotism was nothing unusual in the English Renaissance, his reputation for it was considerable long after his death (see below, p.186); so maybe his four-year absence from what, in 'Upon Appleton House', he was to hail as 'Thou, that dear and happy Isle/The Garden of the World ere while' [p.72], did help to settle his affections firmly upon his own country. His (studied?) failure to leave any substantial reference to his travels seems to endorse this fondness for England. While Marvell was away, his native city of Hull survived two Royalist sieges, during one of which part of the Charterhouse was destroyed; and at Cambridge the parliamentary forces purged college membership of Royalists and Anglicans and their chapels of idolatrous imagery (plate 9). To return to a land divided and hideously mutilated by civil war must have done much ultimately to confirm that alternative 'Idolatry' for his country, with which, after Marvell's death, Halifax was to invest the idea of a 'Trimmer':

he doth not Worship the Sun, because 'tis not peculiar to us, it rambles about the World, and is less kind to us than others; but for the Earth of *England*, tho perhaps inferior to that of many places abroad, to him there is a Divinity in it, and he would rather dye, than see a spire of *English* Grass trampled down by a Foreign Trespasser: He thinketh there are a great many of his mind, for all plants are apt to taste of the Soyl in which they grow, and we that grow here, have a Root that produceth in us a Stalk of English Juice, which is not to be changed by grafting or foreign infusion.

Marvell would have appreciated, above all, Halifax's choice of imagery.

Of Marvell's travels in Holland, France, Italy and Spain there is meagre information in his own writings. About twelve years after his tour he composed a poem on 'The Character of Holland' [pp.100–3], most of which is very general and evinces little obvious first-hand experience of the country. He puns on a few Dutch words, Englishes a few more (hogs, bores, skipper), both of which suggest the linguistic skills that he became known for. He alludes to the habit of carrying stoves to church ('See but their *Mairmaids* with their *Tails of Fish*,/Reeking at *Church* over the *Chafing-Dish*'), which he may therefore have seen for himself; but then he may also be recalling a woodcut of a mermaid sitting in her house from some such book as Guicciardini's *Description de Touts Les Pays-Bas* (Arnhem, 1613, facing p.358). He alludes to the shrine outside The Hague, visited also by John Evelyn in 1641, where a woman reputedly gave birth to 365 children; but this reference may be based on mere tourist hearsay and anyway seems invoked in the poem more as the excuse

9 Destruction of religious images, engraving, 1640s.

for a bad pun at line 66. Of his time in France nothing is recorded. We know he visited Geneva. In Italy we gather only that he passed a hideously boring day with Richard Flecknoe in Rome, probably in 1645–6, when we know that this poetic tormentor was at the English College. This, too, Marvell epitomized in a poem, 'Fleckno, an English Priest at Rome' [pp.87–91], which Augustus Birrell, with admirable restraint, called 'an unsatisfactory *souvenir de voyage*' (p.20). Then, finally, we gather from a letter that he took fencing lessons in Spain:

My Fencing-master in *Spain,* after he had instructed me all he could, told me, I remember, there was yet one Secret, against which there was no Defence, and that was, to give the first Blow.   [II.324]

And since 'Upon Appleton House' alludes to 'the *Toril*/Ere the Bulls enter at Madril' [p.76], we can suppose he also saw some bull-fighting at Madrid.

It has been assumed that Marvell travelled as a tutor to a wealthier gentleman's son. Since he spent some time in the 1650s as tutor, first to Mary Fairfax and then to a ward of Cromwell's, it is argued that he'd already gained the experience that would have recommended him to those important employers. Over fifty years ago Margoliouth discovered an entry in the Pilgrim's Book of the Jesuit English College at Rome under the date 18 December 1645, which recorded the presence there of one 'N. Skinner' and his tutor; the date is certainly right, and the tradition of some responsibility by the Skinner family for Marvell's travels lends support (if only on the principle of no smoke without fire) to the record, since Margoliouth claimed (it now seems wrongly) that N. Skinner stands for 'Ned', the eldest son of Mrs Skinner of Thornton Curtis[22]. Marvell's travelling as a tutor to whomever would certainly provide a plausible explanation of how he was able to afford to maintain himself abroad for four years.

And with that, typically inconclusive, evidence, our knowledge of his European travels peters out. Speculation is never an adequate substitute and its hypotheses can be made to slip dangerously into the status of facts. But, nevertheless, I propose to offer some guesses as to a few of the preoccupations and interests of Marvell's travels, without (it is hoped) falling into the 'sounding words and hyperbolical images' for which another traveller called Marvel is gently mocked in Dr Johnson's *Idler* 49. To guide us in reconstructing Marvell's itineraries and interests along the route we have a considerable literature by other travellers who did commit themselves to paper, either privately, in letters and journals, or publicly in some form of travel book. Since travel was also fairly standardized in those days, we can infer from other documents the scope, motives and excitements of foreign travel that would be relevant to Marvell. The best-known and probably the most valuable of these travel accounts is contained in John Evelyn's 'Kalendarium'. Evelyn (plate 10) was Marvell's senior by one year, and in his journeyings through the Netherlands, France and Italy he drew, obviously, upon his own observations, but also relied extensively, as the modern editor of the *Diary* has been able to show, upon a variety of guide-books and reference works, bits of which were transcribed into his narrative. Evelyn's experiences prove a useful analogue to Marvell's, but I shall follow his example and invoke other travel writings and a variety of contemporary topographical literature wherever it seems particularly useful[23].

Like his modern counterpart, the mid-seventeenth-century traveller went abroad for all sorts of reasons—political, commercial, cultural or educational; to assuage restlessness or curiosity or to escape from boredom, political danger or religious hostility at home. Perhaps the main

10   *John Evelyn*, by Hendrick von der Borcht, 1641.

difference between travel then and now was its difficulty, the physical discomforts and dangers; proportionally, the excitements, privileges and enrichments were, if not greater, more esteemed. Travellers left England on embassies with political or commercial objectives, as Marvell was to do in the 1660s (see below, pp.144–8), or in smaller, private groups, some to prosecute their business interests—Marvell's connections with the port of Hull must have made him attentive to such matters, especially in the Netherlands—some to study languages and sciences or as students of politics: we *know* that Marvell went abroad in the mid 1650s for those reasons (see below, p.132). If we invoke the tradition of Marvell's first journey abroad as a tutor, then he would probably have travelled in a small group, joining other such tutors and their gentlemen pupils as inclinations and the coincidence of routes dictated, and the central purposes of the tour would have been what James Howell, in *Instructions and Directions for Forren Travell*, termed enrolling oneself in 'a moving *Academy*, or the true *Peripatetique School*'[24].

The account that Marvell's future colleague and friend, John Milton, gave of his own travels around Europe in the *Second Defence of the People of England* must partly have coincided with that which the Yorkshireman could have given, both in its itinerary and in the prime motive for setting out in the first place: 'Curiosity . . . to see foreign countries, and above all, Italy'. Political, religious and intellectual encounters along the route were a large means of satisfying Milton's expectations as they must have been of Marvell's, even if the latter did not probably have such distinguished introductions and encounters as the former.

Given Marvell's subsequent poetry and political career it would be safe to assume that Europe held two particularly dominant interests for him: religion and gardens. Foreign religious culture was perpetually fascinating to seventeenth-century Englishmen, who were often obsessed with the novelty of such Catholic countries as France, Italy, Spain and the Spanish Netherlands. Marvell's brief flirtation with Catholicism at Cambridge must have made it a matter of continuing interest, whether disillusioned or still favourable. His later support for religious toleration would have been grounded in these first-hand experiences of religion in different societies. Equally, like many other seventeenth-century Englishmen, he would have been struck by the sophisticated progress in garden design, derived largely from Italy, whereby Europe far surpassed England. Back in Yorkshire after his travels Marvell would recall Aranjuez and Bel Retiro [I.86], two palaces with famous gardens near Madrid, and it seems inconceivable that he should have confined himself to visiting only those two. Among all the booty and souvenirs of travel—books, engravings, pictures, furniture—gardens would necessarily feature only in written or visual descriptions; yet the experience of them survived and was treasured in less tangible forms to reappear in actual English imitations back home, in stage or masque designs or—as in Marvell's case—in the imagery of his poems and his evident habit of understanding the garden world. But, after all, as James Howell noted (p.106), '*Language* is the greatest outward testimony of *Travell*'; and we know for a rare *fact* that Marvell certainly acquired those skills and benefits from his travels abroad.

To leave England, he would have required a Privy Council pass; so, like Evelyn and Peter Mundy, who left for the continent about the same time, he would have presented himself at the Custom House in London before departing. Fleeing what Evelyn called (p.29) 'this ill face of things at home, which gave umbrage to wiser than my selfe' (had Marvell, like Evelyn, witnessed Strafford's execution on 12 May 1641?) the traveller soon faced the rival hazards of winds, tides and hostile foreign shipping between Gravesend and the Dutch coast; the United Provinces were at war with Spain (until 1648) so that vessels tended to travel in convoy.

The Netherlands, according to Howell (p.88), 'have been for many years, as one may say, the very *Cockpit of Christendom, the Schoole of Armes, and Rendez-vous of all adventurous Spirits*'. Leisurely wanderings throughout the United Provinces (the modern Holland) and the Spanish Netherlands (modern Belgium) would have taken Marvell, as it took Evelyn, to all the major cities, some of them several times, thus allowing a full scrutiny of the country's religion and state of war. Evelyn was much excited by the latter and stopped frequently to inspect fortifications, where he often recorded the landscaping of the military sites—'especially the Counterscarp is worthy of note, curiously hedg'd with a quick, and planted with a stately row of Limes on the Ramparts' (Evelyn, p.60). At Antwerp, most especially, was 'the most matchlesse piece of modern Fortification in the World', where nothing 'more ravished me then those delicious shades and walkes of stately Trees, which render the incomparably fortified Workes of the Towne one of the Sweetest places in Europ' (Evelyn, p.67). One wonders if Marvell later came to compare these active fortifications, beautified with gardens in the Netherlands, with Fairfax's gardens in Yorkshire, merely decorated with the imagery of defences:

> when retired here to Peace,
> His warlike Studies would not cease;
> But laid these Gardens out in sport
> In the just Figure of a Fort;
> And with five Bastions it did fence,
> As aiming one for ev'ry Sense.   [p.71]

Travellers were all, inevitably, struck with the landscape of Holland; what Howell described as 'a People planted as it were under the *Sea*, out of

11 *The Martelaarsgracht in Amsterdam,* by J. van der Heyden.

whose jawes they force an habitation' (p.89). What Mundy called 'much low and drowned land' (p.64), Marvell described

> How did they rivet, with Gigantick Piles,
> Thorough the Centre their new-catched Miles;
> And to the stake a strugling Country bound,
> Where barking Waves still bait the forced Ground;
> Building their *watry Babel* far more high
> To reach the *Sea,* then those to scale the *Sky.*   [p.100]

In towns like Amsterdam (plate 11), not only was their tidiness notable, but this strange intermingling of land and sea:

so accommodated with Grafts, Cutts, Sluces, Moles & Rivers, that nothing is more frequent then to see a whole Navy of Marchands & others environ'd with streetes

& houses, every particular mans Barke, or Vessell at anker before his very doore, and yet the Streetes so exactly straite, even, & uniforme that nothing can be more pleasing, especialy, being so frequently planted and shaded with the beautifull lime trees, which are set in rowes before every mans house, affording a very ravishing prospect.   (Evelyn, p.46)

Prominent aspects of Netherlandish culture to strike travellers were its religious variety, its paintings and its gardens. Whether or not Marvell was already in the 1640s committed to religious toleration, he would presumably have shared the common fascination with, what Mundy called, 'A Tolleration here of all sects religion' (p.68). William Brereton at Dort in 1634 observed how 'Arminians, Brownists, and Anabaptists, and Manists, do lurk here and also swarm, but not so much tolerated as at Rotterdam' (p.13). Amsterdam was remarkable for its synagogue and Jewish life; Antwerp, for its Jesuits' 'most sumptuous and most magnificent Church . . . within wholy incrusted with marble inlayed & polish'd into divers representations of histories, Landskips, Flowers &c' (Evelyn, p.63). Peter Paul Rubens, who had died on 30 May 1640, had work at Antwerp and at Brussels that Evelyn admired. Indeed, the English traveller was struck with the Dutch taste for paintings. Evelyn sent home 'Landscips, and Drolleries' (p.39) (landscape is originally a Dutch word), while Mundy observed that

As For the art off Painting and the affection of the people to Pictures, I thincke none other goe beyond them, there having bin in this Country Many excellent Men in thatt Faculty, some att presentt, as Rembrantt, etts, All in general striving to adorne their houses.   (p.70)

Another traveller, Brereton, sent his purchases, including pictures, back to England via a shipman from Marvell's hometown of Hull.

But though the taste for landscape paintings is frequently noticed, it was the Dutch, as we would say 'formal', gardens that were so notable. For one thing, gardens seemed to be everywhere: whether 'particular little gardens' (Mundy, p.75) or larger villas 'built'—as Evelyn said (p.35)—'after the Italian manner'. They afforded a travelling Englishman, especially one like Marvell from the provinces, his first view of the high Renaissance development of garden art; for by the end of the 1630s English gardens had been less radically affected by Renaissance design and were still generally small, having been not long emancipated from the fortified manor house or castle. We see something of the Dutch taste in garden design that Marvell would have encountered in a fairly prosperous household in Ludolf de Jong's picture of a terrace (plate 12): the style is orderly, neat, obviously a gardener's garden; but with the statues decorating the parterre and the vista through into another part of the estate we get a hint of a more Italianate taste. Evelyn, with his lifelong

12   *Garden Terrace*, by Ludolf de Jonge.

absorption in garden theory and practice, is the most eloquent and exciting authority: his Netherlands journal records visits to gardens from his very first day in Flushing (p.31). At Ryswick he saw the country house of the Prince of Orange. At The Hague one of the small gardens attached to the Binnenhof elicited his enthusiasm for its 'close-Walkes, Statues, Marbles, Grotts, Fountaines, and artificiall Musique &c' (p.41). That brief catalogue establishes the range of items that a typical European Renaissance garden offered its visitors; its design would be calculated to display all these features to the best advantage.

The garden experience was, however, not simply a response to the delights of design. It was, equally importantly, the visitor's comprehension of a whole world of meaning couched in visual language of sculpture and other ornaments. At Brussels, for example, Evelyn visited the Cour (pp.71–2), subsequently burnt down in 1731 (the site being now occupied by the Place Royale). Along the terrace above the vineyard were 'the Statues of all the Spanish kings...the opposite Wals paynted by Rubens, being an history of the late tumults in Belgia'. Such deliberate manipulation of a visitor's thoughts by visual imagery, focusing his mind upon the appropriate history of the spot on which he stood, is an essential ingredient of Renaissance gardens; it is often forgotten by literary critics of 'Upon Appleton House', where Marvell properly meditates upon the ruined nunnery and what it tells him of earlier Fairfax history (see below pp.91–4). Sometimes gardens referred visitors to an anthology of classical allusions, as Edward Browne found in a garden at Vianen belonging to the Count of Brederode (pp.21–2), where there were statues of the twelve Caesars and of Aristotle (who had taught among the gardens of the Lyceum outside Athens).

Gardens had always been places of instruction as well as delight. Marvell's own poem, 'The Garden' [pp.51–3], testifies to that. Yet in the light of his visit to the Netherlands Marvell's poem also shows how aware he was of the adjustments that the seventeenth century was to make to man's relationship with the natural world; this involved, above all, a gradual development of an expressive vision at the expense of the emblematic, of an empirical or scientific regard at the expense of the discovery of *a priori* ideas in a garden world. 'The Nymph complaining' shows the poet both, as it were, extrapolating a psychological history from an imagined emblem ('my unhappy Statue shall/Be cut in Marble') and exploring the expressive analogies that the speaker discovers in the natural world around her. 'The Garden' celebrates both an actual and a symbolic world:

> How vainly men themselves amaze
> To win the Palm, the Oke, or Bayes;
> And their uncessant Labours see
> Crown'd from some single Herb or Tree.
> Whose short and narrow verged Shade
> Does prudently their Toyles upbraid;
> While all Flow'rs and all Trees do close
> To weave the Garlands of repose.
>
> Fair quiet, have I found thee here,
> And innocence thy Sister dear!
> Mistaken long, I sought you then
> In busie Companie of Men.
> Your sacred Plants, if here below,
> Only among the Plants will grow.
> Society is all but rude,
> To this delicious Solitude.

Marvell wittily acknowledges what one of his contemporaries, Walter Montague, called the 'holy garden of Speculation'[25]; that is, he invokes the symbolic attributes of plants and the syntax of arcane meanings that they

13 *The Tulip Garden,* by Peter Brueghel the Younger, 1632.

offer. Yet he also recalls us to the garden world as it simply and actually is. He moves, then, in gardens of the sort that the younger Brueghel shows (plate 13), where all is dedicated to horticultural science. Yet he also bears in mind those mental gardens that Henry Hawkins explores in *Partheneia Sacra*, a piece of Jesuit propaganda published one year after Brueghel painted his *Tulip Garden*[26]. The gardens of Hawkins and Brueghel may look the same, but the former's meditations focus upon 'the flowers of all vertues' that flourish only in an emblematic *hortus conclusus* (plate 14). If the tendency of much English thinking was still to register the emblematic or hieroglyphic elements of a garden—what Henry Vaughan announced in his 'I walke the garden, and there see/*Ideas* of his Agonie'—a visit to the Netherlands must have recalled English visitors to the scientific vision. Brereton records that when he visited Leyden University, he attended a class conducted by Adolphus Vorstius and held *in* the physic garden,

THE EMBLEME.

THE POESIE.

The Paufe.

EVE, *like a* Nightingal, *was plac'd to fing*
In Eden, *where, with euerlafting fpring,*
GOD *for her folace pleafant arbours rays'd,*
Had she with lowlie ftraines her MAKER prays'd.
But to an Alt *her mind afpir'd too high,*
Would be like GOD, *affecting* DEITIE.
Therefore from Eden's *fpring she was expel'd,*
Sad Philomel, *to mourne :* Til GOD *beheld*
A Nightingal *with an* exulting ftraine,
That magnifyed her Lord. *But downe againe*
She lowly ftoop'd, & iug'd it, when she fayd:
He hath beheld *euen me* a feruile Mayd.

14   Emblem, engraving from H. Hawkins's *Partheneia Sacra*, 1663.

where he was instructed in the botanical and medicinal properties of the herbs and simples rather than in their arcane and symbolic meanings (p.40).

Marvell's nature poems frequently turn upon these alternative visions of *scientia* and *sapientia*. At the start of 'On a Drop of Dew' we are invited to scrutinize an actual moment of the phenomenal world: the dew drop

> in its little Globes Extent,
> Frames as it can its native Element.
> How it the purple flow'r does slight,
> Scarce touching where it lyes,
> But gazing back upon the Skies,
> Shines with a mournful Light... [p.12]

But that vision is carefully controlled in the interests of a sustaining analogy, which surfaces after eighteen lines as

> So the Soul, that Drop, that Ray
> Of the clear Fountain of Eternal Day,
> Could it within the humane flow'r be seen,
> Remembring still its former height
> Shuns the sweat leaves and blossoms green;
> And, recollecting its own Light,
> Does, in its pure and circling thoughts, express
> The greater Heaven in an Heaven less.

Such 'expressions' of the noumenous via the phenomenal world also occur in 'The Picture of little T.C. in a Prospect of Flowers' [pp.40–1]. This 'nimph' is an apt mirror of Marvell's own conduct, as he keeps his eye steadily upon real gardens and horticultural verities, like Brueghel's, even as he manoeuvres in the speculative gardens of Hawkins or Montague. She 'loves to lie' in the 'green Grass':

> And there with her fair Aspect tames
> The Wilder flow'rs, and gives them names:
> But only with the Roses playes;
> And them does tell
> What Colour best becomes them, and what Smell.

The poet continues by pondering 'for what high cause/This Darling of the Gods was born!' and his final view of her in a delicate prospect of natural imagery seems to ascribe to her the role that is traditionally played by Flora:

> Mean time, whilst every verdant thing
> It self does at thy Beauty charm,
> Reform the errours of the Spring;

Make that the Tulips may have share
Of sweetness, seeing they are fair;
And Roses of their thorns disarm:
    But most procure
That Violets may a longer Age endure.

But O young beauty of the Woods,
Whom Nature courts with fruits and flow'rs,
Gather the Flow'rs, but spare the Buds;
Lest *Flora* angry at thy crime,
To kill her Infants in their prime,
Do quickly make th'Example Yours;
    And, ere we see,
Nip in the blossome all our hopes and Thee.

In such garden and woodland poems Marvell, it seems to me, draws upon a larger, European experience of apprehending the natural world. 'The Picture of little T.C.' reshapes literary traditions[27] by recalling actual gardens. Her jurisdiction over the flowers not only echoes Eve's but those Floras' figured in garden sculpture. Richard Blome's *The Gentleman's Recreation* (1686) shows Flora presiding over her garden (plate 15), just as Marvell imagines little T.C. doing over her flowers. The engraving illustrates not only a basic design of garden stairs descending from one level to another but also that gardenist idea whereby some statue or other representation of the *genius loci* announces to a visitor the particular 'meaning' of the spot he is in. Among that rich hoard of engravings of Holland collected by Christoffel Beudeker and now in the Map Room of the British Library are several views of sections of gardens presided over by some such sculptured image. Marvell's garden poetry, as we shall see again (Chapter 6), is ever aware of these actual and symbolic elements of garden design and ideology. And it would have been in the Netherlands that he first realized their scope.

From the Netherlands Legouis supposes Marvell to have travelled south down the Rhône to Bellegarde, Lyons, Avignon. Evelyn's experience is less useful at this point, because he returned to England from the Spanish Netherlands, setting out again in October 1643 via Dover and Calais. Evelyn used a recently published guidebook, *Le Voyage de France* by Claude de Varennes (1639), upon which Marvell might also have relied. It lists, with some historical information, places and monuments worth visiting.

Evelyn's route was the (still) standard one from Calais, Boulogne, Abbeville and St Denis, to Paris; then, southwards down the Loire, back eastwards to Lyons, whence to Avignon, Marseilles and Cannes, from which Italy was reached by boat. If Marvell did not detour into central France, especially to Paris and its environs, he would presumably have

15 *Flora*, engraving from Richard Blome's *The Gentleman's Recreation*, 1686.

seen much of this when he returned later from Spain. Perhaps that centripetal pull towards Italy—'now to shape my Course so as I might Winter in Italy', as Evelyn himself put it (p.151)—may have been irresistible and the shortest route from the Netherlands therefore deemed the best. At any rate, when Marvell returned to France in 1656, he was described as 'a notable English Italo-Machavillian' [II.378].

In France the consciousness of being in a Catholic country was insistent, whether because 'courteous' Jesuits engaged one in disputations, so that a traveller was advised by Howell to be 'well grounded and settled in his Religion' before venturing into such debates (p.9), or owing to the presence of relics ('one of the Thornes of our Saviours Crowne, & a piece of the real Crosse': Evelyn pp.154–5). The sumptuousness and ornamentation of churches, especially in contrast to the iconoclastic parliamentarians back home, were also remarkable. Besides religion and a study of French politics and institutions, the chief interest of a French visit, especially for persons like Marvell and Evelyn, lay in scientific and academic pursuits. 'Being come into *France*', suggested Howell, 'his best cours will be to retire to some University about the *Loire*, unfrequented by the English' (p.18); which is precisely what Marvell did in the 1650s, when he came as tutor to William Dutton. On his first visit he might have paid a similar visit, perhaps to the University at Montpellier, which 'occupies a special position in the pilgrimage of Englishmen through France and...became prominent at a time when even gentlemen on tour felt anxious to dabble in the sciences'[28]. But there were other modes of exercising a scientific curiosity—exploring the natural phenomena of strange landscapes in the south of France, visiting botanical gardens, such as the famous Jardin des Plantes in Paris, or calling upon scientific amateurs and virtuosi.

Among the delights and stimulations of seventeenth-century travellers, generally lost to modern tourists, were calls upon notable or distinguished men to hear their ideas or to view their collections. We begin to appreciate the fascination with ingenuity, whether in Marvell's poetry or in the contrivance of gardens, when we read about travellers' visits to famous French virtuosi[29]. One of them, Pierre Morin, lived in Paris and entertained his visitors to a dazzling array of engravings, geological and mineral items, flowers, insects and garden design:

The next Morning I was had by a friend to Monsieur Morines Garden; a person who from an ordinary Gardner, is ariv'd to be one of the most skillfull & Curious Persons of France for his rare collection of Shells, Flowers & Insects: His Garden is of an exact Oval figure planted with Cypresse, cutt flat & set as even as a Wall could have form'd it: The Tulips, Anemonies, Ranunculus's, Crocus's &c being of the most exquisite; were held for the rarest in the World, which constantly drew all the Virtuosi of that kind to his house during the season; even Persons of the most illustrious quality: He lived in a kind of Hermitage at one side of his Garden where his Collection of Purselan, of Currall, whereof one is carved into a large Crucifix, is greately estemmed; besids his bookes of Printes, those of Alberts, Van Leydens, Calot &c [i.e. Dürer, Lucas van Leyden, Jacques Callot].   (Evelyn, pp.132–3)

For minds to whom all nature was a scientific as well as a mystical book—Marvell entertains both perspectives in his poetry—the curiosities collected by such virtuosi as Morin (plate 16) offered much for contemplation. Nature's own artifacts, such as shells or precious stones, or man's curious combinations of them into other forms are glanced at in Marvell's 'The Mower against Gardens'—''Tis all enforc'd; the Fountain and the Grot' [p.44]. What the poet's *persona* condenses into such a succinct gesture would have been immediately clear, and with a variety of associations, to a contemporary. The Mower recalls gardens contrived in geometrical shapes, waterworks where that most mobile of natural forms is made to answer the devices of human wit and hydraulic machinery, and the art of topiary, whereby bushes, hedges and trees are cut into fanciful images like that which Brereton discovered near The Hague which 'portraited to the life in box all the postures of a soldier, and a captain on horseback' (p.38). Not far, that, from Fairfax's equally mnemonic flower garden. Such gardenist metamorphoses and other manifestations of human discoveries and intrusions into the natural world were, if not entirely novel experiences for the English traveller like Marvell, at least much more frequently encountered during continental journeys.

The pull of Italy for most travellers was strong; their arrival and journeyings there the culmination of the whole enterprise. But to reach it they had either to cross the Alps or descend—probably by boat down the Rhône to Avignon—to the port of Marseilles. Since the Alpine passes presented to most seventeenth-century travellers a world of horrid and terrifying savagery, it was only the most intrepid or foolhardy that reached Italy through them. In an age when the Derbyshire Peak District struck a writer like Charles Cotton as the work of the Devil, the Alps could only be, to Evelyn (p.509), 'strange, horrid & firefull Craggs & tracts abounding in Pine trees, & onely inhabited with Beares, Wolves, & *Wild Goates*'. His return from Lombardy into Switzerland was dangerous, freezing, frightful, 'melancholy & troublesome' (p.515). We may perhaps assume that Marvell, at least on the outward journey, also avoided such terrors, since he was later to celebrate the 'equal...Hill' at Bilbrough in Yorkshire [I.60–2] and compare its modest curve so favourably to

> Mountains more unjust,
> Which to abrupter greatness thrust,
> That do with your hook-shoulder'd height
> The Earth deform and Heaven fright,
> For whose excrescence ill design'd,
> Nature must a new Center find...

16 *Cabinet of Curiosities,* by Georg Hinz, 1666.

Yet avoiding Alps threw travellers into other dangers, such as 'the Pickaron Turkes who make prize of many small Vessells' along the Riviera (Evelyn, p.166).

At Marseilles English travellers might buy 'Umbrellos against the heate' (Evelyn, p.166) and arrange their onward journey. One of the sights of Marseilles was the galleys and their galley slaves. Evelyn was suitably distressed: 'Their rising forwards, & falling back at their Oare, is a miserable spactacle, and the noyse of their Chaines with the roaring of the beaten Waters has something of strange & fearfull in it' (p.165). A total contrast, that, to the English sailors in the 'remote *Bermudas*' of Marvell's poem [I.17-9]:

> Thus sung they, in the *English* boat,
> An holy and a chearful Note,
> And all the way, to guide their Chime,
> With falling Oars they kept the time.

The Marseilles galley slaves were sent to serenade Evelyn's party by their captain; their 'musique at dinner', however, seems to have pleased.

The *giro d'Italia*, as it was known, was a tour designed to take in as much of the peninsula as possible [30]. In the early years of the century English Protestants had kept mainly to northern Italy—the Veneto and Tuscany—where it was safer for them to travel without fear of the Inquisition. Some intrepid travellers, like the author of that most illuminating document, 'A true Description and Direction of what is most Worthy to be seen in all Italy'[31], ventured to Rome. But even as late as Evelyn's visit there in 1644, a year or two before Marvell's, some care was necessary and Protestants had, for example, to purchase a licence in order to eat meat during Lent. Generally, after 1630, the physical dangers were less and the *giro*, starting from Genoa (reached usually by sea from Marseilles), was routed via Pisa, Lucca and Florence and southwards to Siena and to Rome, which was reached in time for Easter; sometimes this was extended down to Naples, but many travellers returned northwards for Ascensiontide at Venice; thence homewards by Milan, the Simplon and Geneva.

As we have noted, Marvell's Italian journey does yield one rather unsatisfactory document. 'Fleckno, an English Priest at Rome' (see below, pp.53-6). It is a poem full of punning allusions to Catholic customs and beliefs, so Marvell obviously shared other English travellers' distinct awareness of the country's religious ambience. His poem provides a few more hints, as we shall see, of his reactions to the sights, and a few further items may be added from other sources, like the letter to Milton of 1654 which mentions Trajan's Column [II.306]. But otherwise we have to resort to a more contextual sketch of his Italian visit.

Italy, for Howell—and he spoke for every traveller—was variously *'that great limbique of working braines'* and 'the Nurse of Policy, Musique, Architecture, and Limning' (pp.54–5). The country had always fascinated the English with its political life, its political philosophers like Machiavelli, and the variety of its forms of government. One cannot imagine Marvell not being attentive to the various systems and regimes—republics at Lucca and Venice, with the second of which England had always maintained a special relationship, the Duchy of Savoy, the territories of the Florentine Medicis, the Spanish-controlled Lombardy and southern Italy, including Naples, and in the middle the Papal States. As with the prestige of Italy for a political education (and we must not forget that notice of Marvell as an 'Italo-Machavillian'), so with its universities for a scientific one. That of Padua was specially renowned and its registers of this period include the names of innumerable Englishmen: Donne's son was there in 1634, Edmund Waller, straight from over a year's imprisonment by Parliament—a potent reminder of affairs back home—in 1645. Cromwell's personal physician, Laurence Wright, had also matriculated at Padua some years earlier, for it was particularly famed for 'Physic and Anatomie'.

But Italy was perhaps above all a practical and visual education in classics and their modern application—an idea succinctly conveyed in the title of Edmund Warcupp's *Italy in Its Originall Glory, Ruine and Revivall* (1660). For many travellers it was the opportunity to see what they had previously only read about in their Latin texts—thus Thomas Coryat discovered plane trees in the simples garden at Padua, having only seen references to them in 'Vergil and other Authours'[32]. An earlier visitor like George Sandys, translator of Ovid's *Metamorphoses*, obviously saw the classical territories and their surviving ruins through the language of his classical texts: Virgil is used to describe Etna, during his voyage around the Sicilian coast, and Lucretius to explain its geology. Along the shores of the Bay of Naples, so rich in antiquities and memories, Sandys excitedly realizes and relives his studies:

Ciceroes Villa, even at this day so called, where yet do remain the ruines of his Academy, erected in imitation of that of *Athens* (the pleasures whereof he commendeth in his writings:) which he adorned with a schoole, a grove, an open walk, a gallery, and a library...The ruines do show that the buildings were ample...Now all is overgrown with briers: and sheep and goats are pastured where the Muses had once their habitation.   (pp.274–5)

Even the natural beauties of the countryside were 'read' in terms of Roman descriptive poetry, and it is evident that throughout the seventeenth century Englishmen travelled, as Joseph Addison was to do in 1701–3, to compare the 'natural face of the country with the landskips that the poets have given us of it'. The views that Paul Brill drew show the

17 *Month of May: Walking on a Terrace*, pen and wash drawing by Paul Brill, 1598.

activities surrounding a villa in ways that must have seemed simply a
realization of Virgil's *Georgics* or of descriptions of Roman villa life by
Martial and Pliny (plate 17). Modern Italy thus seemed an extension into
new forms of the classical past, especially to minds like Marvell's, which
had already celebrated Charles I in terms of Octavius (see p.26) and
would welcome Cromwell home from Ireland in Horatian tones and with
deliberate echoes of Lucan's *Pharsalia*. Above all, the Roman love of
retirement—a theme Marvell was to work with special freshness—pros-
pered anew in the architecture of Italian Renaissance villas. Sometimes in
Rome modern gardens, like that of Cardinal Montalto, were created
within the fragments of classical remains (plate 18).

The gardens visited during the journey across Europe had merely
hinted at the delights to come in Italy: 'For Their Gardens', wrote
Raymond in the introduction to *Il Mercurio Italico*, 'I dare confidently
avow all Christendom affords none so voluptuous, as those within the
Walls and Territory of Rome'. It is worth insisting upon the emphatic
gardenist component of virtually all recorded visits to Italy by the
mid-seventeenth century, because, though Marvell left no explicit
testimony of any such interest, his mode of composing 'Upon Appleton

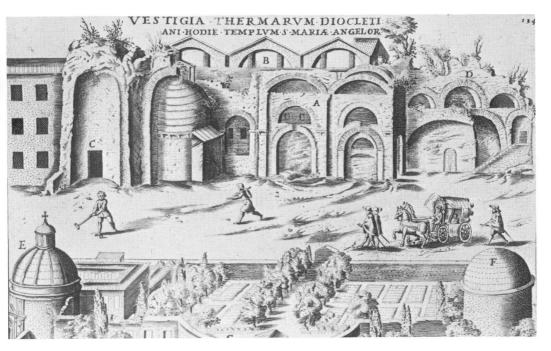

18   Garden in the ruins of Diocletian's Baths, engraving from Jacob Laurus, *Antiquae Urbis Splendor*, 1612.

House'—both the poem and (in his mind) the landscape it celebrates—declares its dependence upon a careful and sensitive absorption of habits learnt in what travellers invariably called 'the Garden of the World' (see below, chapter 6).

The vicinity of Naples (plate 19), which Milton was so pleased to have seen, held out a whole range of delights—a more exotic epitome even than Rome of various elements of the Italian experience. Classical memories crowded fast upon the visitor: even the natural wonders of Vesuvius, which had erupted savagely as recently as 1631, would doubtless have recalled the younger Pliny's account of the disaster of AD 79. What remained of the Lake Avernus after an earthquake of 1538 recalled visits of Ulysses and Aeneas to the underworld, the entrance to which was supposed to have been here. And modern poets, too, were tempted to invoke the strange topography of the Phlegraean Fields for their visions of Hell; Solfatara (plate 20) may have given Milton his imagery of 'penal fire' into which the fallen angels of *Paradise Lost* were consigned[33]:

> The dismal Situation waste and wilde,
> A Dungeon horrible, on all sides round

As one great Furnace flam'd...
and a fiery Deluge, fed
With ever-burning Sulphur unconsum'd.

And regained from this vicious natural world and amid the ruins of a
classical one were the garden paradises, like the Duke of Toledo's
'orchard', decorated with 'many excellent statues' and 'every where

19 *Bird's Eye View of Naples*, by Monsù Desiderio, *c.*1630.

Fountains of fresh water, adorned with Nymphs and Satyres: where the artificial rocks, shells, mosse, and tophas, seem to excell even that which they imitate'[34].

The sculpture, ancient and modern, which featured prominently in

51

20 (top) The Phlegraean Fields, engraving from Marco Sadeler's *Vestigi della Antichitàdi Roma,* 1666.

21 (above) Garden of Casa Galli, drawing by Martin van Heemskerck, 1630s.

Italian gardens, some of which were originally created around collections of them, like the Belvedere Courtyard at the Vatican[35], made its mark at least twice on Marvell's visit. In Martin van Heemskerck's drawing of another sculpture garden, that of the Casa Galli in Rome (plate 21), we see, besides the prominent Michelangelo *Bacchus*, a bas-relief on the wall behind. Such bas-reliefs were *de rigueur* as a feature of any garden, as the rather weary catalogues of Evelyn (pp.234, 240, 286 among other references) or Raymond (pp.77–8) reveal. Marvell himself may have been bored with them too, for his violent frustrations with Richard Flecknoe issue at one point in the image of 'This *Basso Relievo* of a Man'. Heemskerck's drawing also shows on the ground to the left a broken torso of a river god; many of these were recovered during the Renaissance, and either originals or copies served gardens, like those of the Villa Lante at Bagnaia (plate 22), as striking imagery of *genius loci*. Perhaps these, too, were recalled by Marvell, when at Nun Appleton he pictures himself as some such river god, the very essence of an idle retreat along the water meadows:

> Oh what a Pleasure 'tis to hedge
> My Temples here with heavy sedge;
> Abandoning my lazy Side,
> Stretcht as a Bank unto the Tide.   [I.82]

Rome, if only because of the disagreeable chances of travel, obviously made an impression on Marvell. Whether, like John Milton some half a dozen years earlier, he had a stimulating social and intellectual life to compensate for the 'frequent visits' of Flecknoe we do not know. When Marvell in 1654 came to read Milton's *Defensio Secunda* he would have found something of the latter's resort to 'the private academies of Italy, where I was favoured', but nothing of his reception by Cardinal Barberini and the musical and operatic entertainments. At one of these Milton was in the company of Bernini, the baroque sculptor and architect, then at the height of his powers, and at others he heard sing the famous Leonora Baroni, whom he celebrated in three Latin epigrams[36]. Marvell, too, must have encountered some of this life during his stay, but he records only the insufferable poetry-reading and lute-playing of Flecknoe:

> Now as two Instruments, to the same key
> Being tun'd by Art, if the one touched be
> The other opposite as soon replies,
> Mov'd by the Air and hidden Sympathies;
> So while he with his gouty Fingers craules
> Over the Lute, his murmuring Belly calls,
> Whose hungry Guts to the same streightness twin'd
> In Echo to the trembling Strings repin'd.

22   River God at the Villa Lante, Bagnaia, second half of sixteenth century.

Marvell offers him a meal, wrily thinking that by giving him meat he'll be made a Protestant. But before they can descend from Flecknoe's third-floor lodging (a tiny room, where 'who came last is forc'd first to go'), there is an aggressive encounter with another visitor:

> I meet one on the Stairs who made me stand,
> Stopping the passage, and did him demand:

> I answer'd he is here *Sir*; but you see
> You cannot pass to him but thorow me.
> He thought himself affronted; and reply'd,
> I whom the Pallace never has deny'd
> Will make the way here; I said *Sir* you'l do
> Me a great favour, for I seek to go.

The toughness that shows in the Nettleton portrait of Marvell obviously reveals itself here, and in retrospect the violence is transmuted into yet another swipe at Catholicism, for

> I, that was
> Delightful, said there can no Body pass
> Except by penetration hither, where
> Two make a crowd, nor can three Persons here
> Consist but in one substance.

Over the meal 'Poems did and Quarrels cease', only to be renewed once Flecknoe had recharged his energies. Marvell's recollected distaste for the whole encounter returns in some disgusting verses on the poet's habit of retrieving manuscripts from about his person, like a leper's peeling skin or French youths comparing their syphilitic sores. The aggressor of the stairs now takes to reciting Flecknoe's verses, but his praise of them cannot obviate reading them badly:

> But all his praises could not now appease
> The provok't Author, whom it did displease
> To hear his Verses, by so just a curse
> That were ill made condemn'd to be read worse:
> And how (impossible) he made yet more
> Absurdityes in them then were before.
> For he his untun'd voice did fall or raise
> As a deaf Man upon a Viol playes,
> Making the half points and the periods run
> Confus'der then the atomes in the Sun.

The episode ends with Marvell off to hang a painted version of it as a votive offering in St Peter's. Assuming that Marvell wrote the satire some years later in England, we may speculate that he could have been fuelled to the attack by reading in Flecknoe's 1653 volume, *Miscellanea, or poems of all sorts, with divers other pieces* (a title that certainly recalls the impromptu miscellany of that Roman day), a poem on 'Stillborn Silence':

> Stillborn Silence, thou that art
> Flood gate of the deeper heart;
> Offspring of a heavenly kind,

Frost o' the mouth and thaw o' the mind;
Secrecy's confidant, and he
Who makes religion mystery;
Admiration's speaking'st tongue...
...
With thy enthusiasms come,
Seize our tongues, and strike us dumb.

That rather touching and fine poem must have been in ironic contrast to
the silence Marvell had wished for in vain a decade or so earlier.

From Italy he went to Spain, by boat maybe, or along the French coast.
For a slightly later traveller, Francis Willughby[37], it was a depressing
country, not usually included in itineraries: the University of Valencia was
backward, with no new books; the countryside desolate, though
interesting enough to the minerologist and natural historian; the people
were lazy, uncivil to strangers, and the 'most orthodox and rigid *Romanists*
in the world'. That there were compensations for Marvell we may assume:
the instruction in fencing, the gardens (Moorish near Seville, Italianate
around the Escurial), perhaps the bull-fighting (though Willughby
compared it with Roman heathenism). After Italy it must have been
strange to see so little villa life, for, at least according to Peacham, 'the
Gentry affect not the Country, but desire to live in walled Townes
altogether'. And if Willughby again was correct that 'For fornication and
impurity they are the worst of all Nations', Marvell was probably relieved
to escape into France and thus to England once again.

5 Muses Dear & the Arts of Pow'r

Upon his return Marvell established new contacts and renewed old ones
with Royalist friends. This seems evident from his publications of 1649:
one is an elegy 'Upon the Death of Lord Hastings' [I.4–5], the other, the
poem contributed, along with offerings by a dozen of Lovelace's friends,
to that Cavalier poet's *Lucasta*. Another, even more Royalist poem, 'An
Elegy upon the Death of my Lord Francis Villiers' [I.429–32], may also be
Marvell's.

'To his Noble Friend, Mr Richard Lovelace' [pp.2–4] was addressed to one already out of fortune and out of favour:

> The Ayre's already tainted with the swarms
> Of Insects which against you rise in arms.
> Word-peckers, Paper-rats, Book-scorpions,
> Of wit corrupted, the unfashion'd Sons.
> The barbed Censurers begin to looke
> Like the grim consistory on thy Booke;
> And on each line cast a reforming eye,
> Severer then the yong Presbytery.

A rather fuzzy parliamentary conceit is evolved out of an earlier episode in Lovelace's career, when in 1642 he had been imprisoned after presenting a petition to the House of Commons on the King's behalf from the County of Kent, although a previous one had been publicly burnt. But the poem's main success in the celebratory vein is the fantasy of Lovelace's mistresses rushing, 'though yet undrest', to defend their admirer against the presbyters. One of them even mistakes Marvell for an adversary. It could be no more than a well-contrived dénouement for the poem; but it also draws attention to the poet's not entire identification with the Cavalier mode in either costume or verse. The ladies are reassured—

> O no, mistake not, I reply'd, for I
> In your defence, or in his cause would dy.

The poet's riposte has all the makings of Cavalier tone and manner, even perhaps to a smutty innuendo; it is as if Marvell wished to draw Lovelace's attention to his commitment to, even while establishing his detachment from, the role. It is the first of many hints that Marvell was agile and practised in absorbing local colour, in merging into the local landscape, while at the same time showing us what he was up to. His final apostrophe to Lovelace, 'Him, valianst men, and fairest Nymphs, approve', is however an entirely appropriate tribute to the author of 'To Lucasta, Going to the Warres', to which other oblique allusions are made:

> Tell me not (Sweet) I am unkinde,
>   That from the Nunnerie
> Of thy chaste breast, and quiet minde,
>   To Warre and Armes I flie.
>
> True; a new Mistresse now I chase,
>   The first Foe in the Field;
> And with a stronger Faith imbrace
>   A Sword, a Horse, a Shield.

> Yet this Inconstancy is such,
>   As you too shall adore;
> I could not love thee (Deare) so much,
>   Lov'd I not Honour more.

The contrast in tone, style and manner between Lovelace's lucid lyrics and Marvell's unsinging, pragmatic voice is surely deliberate, a measure of the 'degenerate' times.

Throughout the lyrics that are generally supposed to have been written during these years between Marvell's return from his European travels and his departure to the Fairfaxes' house in Yorkshire about 1650–1 we may trace a similar strategy to that practised towards Lovelace. It involves the assimilation of many poetic themes, styles and imagery of the 1640s. It is a chameleon poetry that takes its protective colouring, as J.B. Leishman has shown, from a wide and attentive scrutiny of contemporary work by Carew, Waller, Crashaw, Cowley, Cleveland and Lovelace himself, as well as from any number of older traditions[38]. His poetry is, then, along with his lust as he boasts in 'To his Coy Mistress', an 'ecchoing Song'. But the acceptance and exploitation of his borrowings sound distinctly individual notes: sometimes in attending to balance, antithesis, proportion, detachment; sometimes in registering the difficulties and the violence of human life. He writes in 'Fleckno'—

> Who should commend his Mistress now? Or who
> Praise him? both difficult indeed to do
> With truth.   [p.91]

Taken out of their context the lines could announce what Marvell's other poetry often implies: though it does not insist that the times were much disturbed and matters of huge moment were in constant question, his poetry suggests the need and the value of judgement and discrimination.

This is not to say that the best of the Cavalier poems do not also display such qualities, but that they seem to do so from a less abstracted perspective than Marvell's thoughtfulness:

> My Love is of a birth as rare
> As 'tis for object strange and high:
> It was begotten by despair
> Upon Impossibility.

> Magnanimous Despair alone
> Could show me so divine a thing,
> Where feeble Hope could ne'er have flown
> But vainly flapt its Tinsel Wing.

> And yet I quickly might arrive
> Where my extended Soul is fixt,
> But Fate does Iron wedges drive,
> And alwaies crouds it self betwixt.   [p.39]

It is, certainly, an extreme example of his exploration of abstractions; unlike other 'Metaphysicals' he seems less concerned with introspection and psychological dramas. Yet the realizing of abstractions (tinsel wing; iron wedges), the quick apprehension of opposites and contraries, even his muted register of violence later in the poem, all 'define' a love that hides particular and intense emotions beneath the studied conceptualism:

> Therefore the Love which us doth bind,
> But Fate so enviously debarrs,
> Is the Conjunction of the Mind,
> And Opposition of the Stars.

Such tensions inform other poems. With 'The Definition of Love' it is particularly tempting for a biographer to fall in with the suggestion, most recently advanced by F.W. Bateson[39], that here Marvell talks of his love for some particular, perhaps Royalist, lady, separated from him by political or social differences. The slight allusions to recent events in such language as 'power', 'decrees', or 'some new convulsion' lend the notion some support, as does the evident intensity of feeling. But the poem's energy consists, just as evidently, in translating any actual personal involvement into a poetic 'object strange and high'. All the biographer can conclude is that the poet, echoing earlier lyrics by Donne, Carew and Lovelace, *disguises* his life resolutely in his art.

There is for Marvell an unusually dramatic tone in 'To his Coy Mistress' [pp.27–8], but it is the drama of argument, as the syllogistic structure of his address shapes the theme:

> If there were infinite time...
> But our life is short...
> Therefore, we must seize the moment...

It is an ancient theme. Catullus sang it, Ben Jonson gave it exquisite English airs ('Come my CELIA, let us prove,/While we may, the sports of love'), and his successors rehearsed it. Edmund Waller's lovely song ('Goe lovely Rose,/Tell her that wastes her time and me') blends feeling, honesty and sophistication. His manner is always easy, conventional, but not without concern:

> Phyllis! why should we delay
> Pleasures shorter than the day
> Could we (which we never can)

> Stretch our lives beyond their span,
> Beauty like a shadow flies,
> And our youth before us dies.
> Or would youth and beauty stay,
> Love hath wings, and will away.
> Love hath swifter wings than Time;
> Change in love to heaven does climb.
> Gods, that never change their state,
> Vary oft their love and hate...

Marvell's tone is sharper and his deepest note is characteristically reserved for a potent realization of an abstraction (Time), in which a bawdy usage ('quaint Honour' = female pudendum) both observes the libertine mode of speech and yet belies its nonchalance:

> But at my back I alwaies hear
> Times winged Charriot hurrying near:
> And yonder all before us lye
> Desarts of vast Eternity.
> Thy Beauty shall no more be found;
> Nor, in thy marble Vault, shall sound
> My ecchoing Song: then Worms shall try
> That long preserv'd Virginity:
> And your quaint Honour turn to dust;
> And into ashes all my Lust.
> The Grave's a fine and private place,
> But none I think do there embrace.

There the negative aspects of the minor premise (that time is short) are found grotesque expression, which approaches burlesque in the final movement of the argument:

> Now let us sport us while we may;
> And now, like am'rous birds of prey,
> Rather at once our Time devour,
> Than languish in his slow-chapt pow'r.
> Let us roll all our Strength, and all
> Our sweetness, up into one Ball:
> And tear our Pleasures with rough strife,
> Thorough the Iron gates of Life.
> Thus, though we cannot make our Sun
> Stand still, yet we will make him run.

What are typical of Marvell there are the concrete figure of pleasure, its endemic violence ('am'rous birds of prey', etc.) and the translation of personal experience, without loss, into a conscious play with literary traditions.

23 *Lucasta*, engraving by William Faithorne after Lely, 1649.

His is a temperament capable of temporary acquiescence in its present circumstances: it tolerated Flecknoe at the time; it acknowledged the iconic postures of Cavalier nonchalance and valour, which Sir Peter Lely so exactly captured (plate 23), when addressing Lovelace—

> Whose hand so rudely grasps the steely brand,
> Whose hand so gently melts the Ladies hand.

And in a poem like 'Daphnis and Chloe' [pp.35–9] Marvell can ape the Cavalier's easy moral line as well as his military know-how:

> He, well read in all the wayes
> By which men their Siege maintain,
> Knew not that the Fort to gain
> Better 'twas the Siege to raise.

But somewhere the poet will temperamentally part company with the mode he employs, as when Daphnis' speech seems to warn against a too easy or conventional sensuality:

> Gentler times for Love are ment.
> Who for parting pleasure strain
> Gather Roses in the rain,
> Wet themselves and spoil their Sent.

It is a habit of mind eager and apt to get involved (we might recall the tradition of his sudden conversion to Catholicism, or, in a different fashion, his impulsive climb of all those stairs to call upon Flecknoe). But it is also a mind quick, perhaps over-sensitive, to register the constraints upon instinct and impulse. These curbs and checks may come from the outer, rival world of public life (these lyrics are shot through with political and military terms), from a ready training in defending a thesis '*Pro* or *Con*', or from a keen sense of the pressures of literary tradition upon his individual talents.

A poem like 'The unfortunate Lover' [pp.29–31] begins by recalling an old-fashioned Garden of Love:

> Alas, how pleasant are their dayes
> With whom the Infant Love yet playes!
> Sorted by pairs, they still are seen
> By Fountains cool, and Shadows green.

Moving, then, into some stanzas that borrow from a more up-to-date and mannerist tradition, emblem books like Otto van Veen's *Amorum Emblemata* (plate 24), or Crispin de Passe's *Thronus Cupidinis*, Marvell becomes grotesque and hilarious:

24 Emblem ('The Ship of Love in Travail'), engraving from Otto van Veen's *Amorum Emblemata*, 1608.

> 'Twas in a Shipwrack, when the Seas
> Rul'd, and the Winds did what they please,
> That my poor Lover floting lay,
> And, e're brought forth, was cast away:
> Till at the last the master-Wave
> Upon the Rock his Mother drave;
> And there she split against the Stone,
> In a *Cesarian Section.*

Part of the poem's 'infected wit', to use Marvell's term to Lovelace, lies in the violence of unfortunate love combined with a sense of its elaborate artifice—it is imaged as emblems, a 'masque', a fencing-match, and the lover expires into music, fiction and heraldic devices:

> dying leaves a Perfume here,
> And Musick within every Ear:
> And he in Story only rules,
> In a Field *Sable* a Lover *Gules.*

25 Studiolo for Francesco de' Medici, by Giorgio Vasari and his circle, 1570–5.

The symbolisms and the self-consciousness of their use are all of a piece with the court masques of Charles I. Marvell obviously relishes this artifice for the scope it affords his detached scrutiny, just as the King could watch at a masque the studied emblems of his own magnificence.

Marvell glances at this courtly world again in 'The Gallery'. Charles had brought off the rather grandiose purchase (for £25,000) of the Duke of Mantua's collection of pictures, though it was itself broken up and sold by Parliament in July 1650. Marvell's poem was written after, or altered to fit, that latter event: 'a Collection choicer far/Then or *White-hall's*, or *Mantua's* were'. He could not have failed at some point on his travels to have seen similar galleries; what Sir Henry Wotton called 'Pinacotheciae... certain Repositaries for workes of rarity in Pictura or other Arts, by the Italians called Studioli'[40]. One such *studiolo* that Marvell might have seen was the tiny closet created by Vasari for Francesco de' Medici in 1570 (plate 25); its walls are covered with bronzes and exquisite paintings, including portraits of women and allegorical and mythical subjects such as Marvell invokes for the pictures of his Clora. The rarefied, claustrophobic little room into which Francesco could have shut himself away is the three-dimensional counterpart of Marvell's gallery, where he contemplates the several lodgings of his soul.

Clora's variousness—murderess and shepherdess, benign like Aurora (Dawn) and crafty like a witch—mirrors Marvell's own delight in antitheses, antinomies, contradictions and paradox. He makes the dialogue form, for example, peculiarly his own in the 1640s as later in the 1650s while at Eton; true, 'A Dialogue between Thyrsis and Dorinda' [pp.19–21] seems readily to have lost its dialectical nature in the hands of a Royalist musician, William Lawes (brother of the more famous Henry), whose setting has come down to us in manuscript[41] (plate 26). This suggests, for one thing, how well and unsubtly Marvell's Cavalier role passed muster among the Royalists. It also reminds us how precarious are the verbal tones that identify scepticism or variety, how easily lost by translation into song. His epigrammatic style in such poems as 'Mourning' [pp.33–5] or 'Eyes and Tears' [pp.15–17] nicely observes the variousness of human motive, yet without the fragmentary effects of Cowley from whom he borrows. His keen discriminations of Clora's reasons for weeping in 'Mourning' are but a corollary of his delight in registering congruence. To isolate for Marvell is also often to blend:

> How wisely Nature did decree,
> With the same Eyes to weep and see!
> That, having view'd the object vain,
> They might be ready to complain.
>
> And, since the Self-deluding Sight,
> In a false Angle takes each hight;

26   Manuscript setting of Marvell's 'A Dialogue between Thyrsis and Dorinda', from Music Book of William Lawes, 1640s (?).

These Tears which better measure all,
Like wat'ry Lines and Plummets fall.

And the force of that lovely poem, 'The Fair Singer' [p.33], lies partly in the acknowledgement of separate 'Beauties ... Joyning ... in fatal Harmony', for 'she with her Eyes my Heart does bind,/She with her Voice might captivate my Mind'. The argument of its second stanza is characteristically Marvellian, for the poet declares his fascination with the singer's complex attraction for him and the compelling *notion* of being fettered by what is insubstantial:

I could have fled from One but singly fair:
My dis-intangled Soul it self might save,
Breaking the curled trammels of her hair.
But how should I avoid to be her Slave,
Whose subtile Art invisibly can wreath
My Fetters of the very Air I breath?

It is yet another occasion upon which one is tempted to talk of Marvell's 'playfulness' with literary tradition and his own situation. 'Play', however, must involve not only the casual or careless meaning of recreation or toying with, though Marvell suggests that motive, but the more strenuous role-playing of theatrical art and psychological involvement. He realizes and can relish the courtly play—it satisfies both a dramatic instinct and a compulsion to become involved; yet he must play on his own terms of detachment and poetical inventiveness. Both are shown to an astonishing degree in the Nymph's lament for her fawn (though it is probably a later poem): like 'The unfortunate Lover', a traditional sorrow (ladies' for dead pets) is led through verses that exactly capture the girl's turmoil into a subtle register of yet more human variousness: the marriage of innocent gaiety (lines 37–70) *and* an intense death wish that follows the recognition of a love larger than the earth allows.

Marvell's disposition to manysidedness, his love of relying upon what John Sherman in Trinity College Chapel termed 'a conjectural descant where we cannot find a certain demonstration'[42], may be part of his make-up or his reaction to the late 1640s. The Civil War not only forced Englishmen to 'take sides' in the most obvious and hateful way, but it required of them endless decisions upon intricate and difficult matters: in religion—Presbyterianism, Independence (sectarianism), re-establishment of a modified Anglican Church; in politics—monarchism, republicanism, military rule, parliamentary rule with some form of liaison with the King. In such circumstances it is just as natural for intelligent and thoughtful men like Marvell to insist upon the variety of options, the truth of each side of a question, as to opt strenuously for one or (which was not the same thing, as Fairfax showed) vigorously reject another.

Something of these often brutal debates is suggested in the imagery of politics ('Tyrannick pow'r depose', '*Democratick* Stars') and war that occurs in these poems. 'The Fair Singer' blandly invokes the indecisiveness of military encounters to stress by contrast the ease of the singer's triumph over the poet:

> It had been easie fighting in some plain,
> Where Victory might hang in equal choice,
> But all resistance against her is vain,
> Who has th'advantage both of Eyes and Voice,
> And all my Forces needs must be undone,
> She having gained both the Wind and Sun.

Yet the only two *published* poems of these years (that for Lovelace's volume and that on Hastings' death) declare a more straightforward attitude, Royalist and elegiacal. Perhaps he reserved tergiversations for private purposes, but the Royalist declarations jibe perfectly with his move to Yorkshire in 1650 or 1651 to serve in the household of Sir Thomas Fairfax, who had disapproved of the trial of Charles I, whose wife had shouted from the public gallery during the trial that Cromwell was a traitor, and who retreated with his family to Nun Appleton to await a restored monarchy. During the last few years of the 1640s political and personal considerations must have changed almost daily; nevertheless, there lies some long-term consistency in Marvell's Royalist leanings.

In the second half of 1649, that is, after the King's execution, Marvell joined thirty-two other poets (including Herrick and Dryden) in elegies for Lord Hastings. There is some strain in his first eight lines, probably no more than usual on such occasions. But Marvell is not averse to alluding to the troubled times:

> Therefore the *Democratick* Stars did rise,
> And all that Worth from hence did *Ostracize*.
>   . . .
> So he, not banisht hence, but there confin'd,
> There better recreates his active Minde.

The second couplet affords another instance of Marvell's quickness at identifying the advantages of antithetical states, with the contemplative opportunities of a heavenly retreat being hailed as a form of activism.

Hastings had died of smallpox, on the eve of his marriage to the daughter of the late king's physician. The previous year Lord Francis Villiers had been killed in a skirmish. The elegy for him exists at Worcester College, Oxford, in a manuscript, not Marvell's, but annotated by George Clarke (1660–1736), probably correctly, as by him. Villiers' direct involvement with the wars bears upon the tone of the elegy, which opens with a reprimand to Fame which

> should not have brought the news
> Thou canst discourse at will and speak at large:
> But wast not in the fight nor durst thou charge.

It is this activism of Villiers (as opposed, there, to the passive messenger-role of Fame) that is applauded and his example enjoined upon his mourners at the end:

> Such are the Obsequies to *Francis* own:
> He best the pompe of his owne death hath showne.
> And we hereafter to his honour will
> Not write so many, but so many kill.
> Till the whole Army by just vengeance come
> To be at once his Trophee and his Tombe.

It has been argued by Wallace (p.30) that Marvell's animus against the army ('heavy *Cromwell*', 'long-deceived *Fairfax*') reveals his 'allegiance to Parliament and the hopes of a treaty' between King Charles I and the Commons. But the poem declares nothing of that discriminating hope. If anything, it rather enjoys its outright enthusiasm, even ensuring some play on the side with rival Cavalier loyalties ('The last and greatest Monarchy of Love').

If anything, the avowedly Royalist stance of the Villiers 'Elegy' is more in line with Marvell's (much later) confession that 'a man finds himself inclinable to favor the weaker party' [Grosart, IV.122]. Such inclinations certainly show themselves briefly in his most famous poem of these years, 'An Horatian Ode upon Cromwel's Return from Ireland' [pp.91–4], as he reviews the events of 1647–50. But concern for the weaker party cannot preclude indefinitely a much stronger admiration for the successes of strength, as Villiers' earlier or Cromwell's now:

> And, if we would speak true,
>   Much to the Man is due.
> Who, from his private Gardens, where
> He liv'd reserved and austere,
>   As if his highest plot
>   To plant the Bergamot,
> Could by industrious Valour climbe
> To ruine the great Work of Time,
>   And cast the Kingdome old
>   Into another Mould.

Cromwell (plate 27) has never been an easy character to read[43]. Marvell's poem captures the complexity of motive and event that made for that enigma. Cromwell emerged into public prominence entirely as a result of

27 *Oliver Cromwell,* by Sir Peter Lely, *c.*1653.

the war. The poet maybe glances at his own position in the opening lines
of the 'Ode', but he is equally right to suggest that it was Cromwell's
'genius as a soldier [that] was to make him the arbiter of England's
destiny' (C.V. Wedgwood):

> 'Tis time to leave the Books in dust,
> And oyl th'unused Armours rust:
>   Removing from the Wall
>   The Corslet of the Hall.

So restless *Cromwel* could not cease
In the inglorious Arts of Peace,
    But through adventrous War
    Urged his active Star.

Cromwell's active recruiting and training of a troop of horsemen, expanded later into a regiment and deployed with such consummate skill and opportunism at Marston Moor in 1644, were the basis of his power. His loyalties to this army often conflicted with his role as a Member of Parliament and with his dedication to working through it, as we see in the march upon London in August 1647, which put the Presbyterians to flight, quelled the riots they had instigated among the apprentices and reinstated the Independent Members of the Commons. He himself came to doubt whether such a show of force against the army's parliamentary opponents was really wise: 'What we gain in a free way is better than twice so much in a forced way'. To such a *Putsch* against his own side—he had also acted earlier that same year to secure the King as the army's as opposed to the Parliament's prisoner—Marvell may well allude in the lines

And, like the three-fork'd Lightning, first
Breaking the Clouds where it was nurst,
    Did thorough his own Side
    His fiery way divide.

No simple invocation of specific event can elucidate this intricate poem, where Marvell's poise allows much diversity of suggestion to inhabit its lines; but it is worth insisting that Marvell has his eye upon contemporary politics and personalities as well as upon contriving the 'color romanus' of the ode[44]. Cromwell occasionally *did* have to exert himself against what at other times—so volatile was the situation—could be counted as 'his own Side'. On another point: Cromwell's militarism was sustained by an indomitable sense of 'election'—after Marston Moor he exclaimed, 'God made them as stubble to our swords', and after Naseby, 'This is none other but the hand of God'. Marvell's lines

Then burning through the Air he went,
And Pallaces and Temples rent:
    And *Caesars* head at last
    Did through his Laurels blast.
'Tis Madness to resist or blame
The force of angry Heavens flame

may well glance at this strong conviction of Cromwell's that God's will worked through him. But the growing impression of the first forty-odd lines is of Cromwell's forceful move to influence and then to fill a power vacuum, created by the King's incompetence and deviousness on the one hand and by the parliamentary and military dissensions on the other:

> Though Justice against Fate complain,
> And plead the antient Rights in vain:
>> But those do hold or break
>> As Men are strong or weak.
> Nature that hateth emptiness,
> Allows of penetration less:
>> And therefore must make room
>> Where greater Spirits come.

Marvell subscribed evidently to the current rumours that Cromwell connived at the King's escape from Hampton Court to the Isle of Wight, where he was again imprisoned in Carisbrooke Castle. These politic manoeuvres are detachedly noted as augmenting his military skills:

> What Field of all the Civil Wars,
> Where his were not the deepest Scars?
>> And *Hampton* shows what part
>> He had of wiser Art.
> Where, twining subtile fears with hope,
> He wove a Net of such a scope,
>> That *Charles* himself might chase
>> To *Caresbrooks* narrow case.

Since Charles's escape did contribute to his eventual trial and execution, to which Marvell next turns, the folklore of Cromwell's part in its connivance strengthens the thesis of his strong manipulation of events. But 'wiser Art', while recalling us to one of the poet's favourite themes, that of contemplation versus activism, nevertheless carries some undertow of scepticism about the wisdom of either machiavellianism or even believing gossip.

Marvell's lines upon Charles I are notable both for their fairness and for their analysis. The King at his trial (plate 28) refused to recognize the authority of the Court of Justice in Westminster and until his last moments upon the scaffold argued that by denying its legality he was shielding his subjects from arbitrary power. Marvell suggests that and much more:

> That thence the *Royal Actor* born
> The *Tragick Scaffold* might adorn:
>> While round the armed Bands
>> Did clap their bloody hands.
> *He* nothing common did or mean
> Upon that memorable Scene:

28 *Charles I at his Trial*, by Edward Bower, 1649.

29 Execution of Charles I, Dutch engraving, 1649.

> But with his keener Eye
> The Axes edge did try:
> Nor call'd the *Gods* with vulgar spight
> To vindicate his helpless Right,
> But bow'd his comely Head,
> Down as upon a Bed.

The execution took place outside the Banqueting House in Whitehall, as a contemporary Dutch engraving shows (plate 29), and Marvell suggests the particular aptness of such a setting by his theatrical imagery. The Banqueting House, designed by Inigo Jones for James I, and decorated under his successor with Rubens's *Apotheosis of James I* (plate 30), epitomized much of Stuart monarchy. Its architecture was Italianate, startlingly handsome in comparison with the rest of the Palace of Whitehall; its painted ceiling announced the royal patronage of the best among contemporary European artists. The ceiling's theme and the elaborate masques presented beneath it (until 1635, when Charles feared that smoke would damage Rubens's canvases) all glorified the monarchy.

The last masque that Inigo Jones, with William Davenant, had created for the court was *Salmacida Spolia*, just over nine years before the execution, on 21 January 1640. Both King and Queen took part; the splendour and cost were unprecedented, the wilful disregard of the gathering constitutional crisis as extraordinary as the wistful thinking of the masque's political message. Charles played his familiar role of Divine Monarch, Philogenes, or lover of his people, though this time with some distinct allusions to martyrdom, for the proscenium opening was decorated with, among other customary virtues, attributes of Christ, Innocence and Forgetfulness of Injuries, to which the King was still appealing at his death. The discord of 'Adverse times' is represented in the masque by a 'horrid scene. . . of storm and tempest', which changed miraculously into a 'landscape. . . as might express a country in peace, rich and fruitful'. A chariot in the sky brings the Good Genius of Great Britain

30 *Apotheosis of James I*, engraving (1720) by Simon Gribelin after Ruben's Banqueting House ceiling (1622).

and Concord into this benign setting, and together they celebrate the King:

> O who but he could thus endure
> To live and govern in a sullen age,
> When it is harder far to cure
> The People's folly than resist their rage?

Philogenes and the Queen, sent down from Heaven by Pallas as his reward, are finally vouchsafed 'a vision of their own ideal reign, 'magnificent buildings' beyond which we see 'a great city' (plate 31). This marvellous illusionistic world, organized by intricate machinery and all the contrivances of costumes, lights, music and poetry, affirmed the royal power, which itself soon proved to belong to a similar world of appearances. In and out of masques, in life and at death, as Marvell says, the King acted his role, though soon after *Salmacida Spolia* some of its other noble actors had sought the parliamentary cause. Charles had ruled, as Stephen Orgel writes, 'according to a political theory that had the quality of a hermetic allegory. In a very profound way the stage at Whitehall was his truest kingdom, the masque the most accurate expression of his mind'[45].

The King's last appearance, then, as '*Royal Actor*' was outside his Banqueting House in the exceedingly cold weather of 30 January 1649. Marvell's economical allusions to the scene and to its symbolical effect alert the reader to a whole background against which Charles's behaviour is both judged and appreciated. He is still play-acting; but he is adopting a truly courageous attitude; the role of divinely appointed monarch is an 'act'; yet it is one that has (or had) political reality. The King, we know, prepared himself rigorously for his final appearance. The tradition that a friend of Marvell's, James Harrington, was on the scaffold and reported matters to him cannot be credited; but the details of the scene soon became common property and Royalist mythology. By another apt coincidence the Bishop of London, Juxon, comforted the King in his last moments, according to John Rushworth's *Historical Collections* (1659), by remarking 'There is but one stage more. This stage is turbulent and troublesome: it is a short one...' Juxon was, of course, relying upon the sense of stage as 'section of a journey'; but his words lent themselves unintentionally to sustain the dramatic scene. And a contemporary print shows Charles upon the scaffold, gesturing like an actor to groups on the right and the left amid carefully disposed properties such as his discarded cloak and the prepared coffin. The King's father, James I, had written that 'A King is as one set on a stage, whose smallest actions and gestures, all the people gazingly doe behold'. And so they did outside the Banqueting House. The royal performance was immaculate, and 'the

31 Set design for *Salmacida Spolia*, by John Webb after Inigo Jones, 1640s.

armed Bands/Did clap their bloody hands'. Regicides applauding their foul deed or moved against their better judgements by Charles's fine 'Scene'? Marvell calmly allows both explanations. It was, above all for a political realist, 'that memorable Hour/Which first assur'd the forced Pow'r'.

Writing his 'Ode' possibly in the early summer of 1650, Marvell placed that lamentable event in a larger political perspective (he had a lively interest in optical relativities—see 'Eyes and Tears' [p.15], stanza ii). In Charles's death 'the *State*/Foresaw it's happy Fate'. And Cromwell's loyal service to the new republic in suppressing the Royalist threats in Ireland further confirmed or 'assur'd' the state's power. The poem moves now more urbanely towards its peroration:

> And now the *Irish* are asham'd
> To see themselves in one Year tam'd:
> So much one Man can do,
> That does both act and know.

77

They can affirm his Praises best,
And have, though overcome, confest
   How good he is, how just,
   And fit for highest Trust:
Nor yet grown stiffer with Command,
But still in the *Republick's* hand:
   How fit he is to sway
   That can so well obey,
He to the *Commons Feet* presents
A *Kingdome,* for his first years rents:
   And, what he may, forbears
   His Fame to make it theirs:
And has his Sword and Spoyls ungirt.
To lay them at the *Publick's* skirt.

Critics like to discover ironies there: first, because the Irish, ruthlessly eliminated at Drogheda, could scarcely, it is suggested, 'affirm his Praises best'; second, that the poem hints at Cromwell's ambition with its '*still* in the Republick's hand' (my italics). Neither seems very plausible. Marvell has other doubts to resolve, as we shall see, besides Cromwell's ambitions to be more than a successful general and the Lord Lieutenant of Ireland. And the Irish campaign was warmly received in London by members of the Council of State, who foresaw similar troubles brewing on their Scottish flanks, and the poem seems to read Cromwell's military successes from their viewpoint. Or is it that the Irish are imagined as learning from their conqueror's 'tolerance' in larger matters? We know that Cromwell, more dedicated to efficiency than ideology, employed former Royalists in Ireland (and Marvell, in celebrating him, is just another). He was also accompanied on the expedition by John Owen as his chaplain, and it is perhaps wise to recall, as Maurice Ashley does, that Owen's sermon to Parliament on the day after Charles's execution was expanded into a pamphlet with the title, *A Discourse about Toleration and the Duty of the Civil Magistrate.* Toleration and civil magistracy were Cromwell's concerns, and Marvell seems to echo them, even if he also stresses the military means to those ends. Cromwell's success in Ireland would be repeated in Scotland, where the ode in prophetic vision follows him against the Covenanters who had come to terms with Charles II (aged twenty) and looked likely to crown him King of the Scots:

   The *Pict* no shelter now shall find
   Within his party-colour'd Mind;
      But from this Valour sad
      Shrink underneath the Plad:
   Happy if in the tufted brake
   The *English Hunter* him mistake;

> Nor lay his Hounds in near
> The *Caledonian* Deer.

The poem then ends on a more discriminating note. Toleration on the poet's part, too, is required and discovered:

> But thou the Wars and Fortunes Son
> March indefatigably on:
>   And for the last effect
>   Still keep thy Sword erect:
> Besides the force it has to fright
> The Spirits of the shady Night,
>   The same *Arts* that did *gain*
>   A *Pow'r* must it *maintain.*

The soldiers of Cromwell's army had said as much themselves a few years before, affirming that they were not a 'mere mercenary Army, hired to serve any arbitrary power of a state, but called forth...to the defence of their own and the people's just rights and liberties'. The poet who returned a Royalist from his European tour had also returned a loyalist. Since by 1650 Cromwell was so evidently not an arbitrary power (did not the Irish affirm as much, and *they* should know?) and since his forays to west and to north were dedicated to sustaining at least a *de facto* state, Marvell lends him support. (A qualified support, nevertheless, for the poem was never published till after the poet's death, and even then it survives in only two copies of *Miscellaneous Poems*, having been cancelled from all the others.) Furthermore, the poet cannot altogether eliminate his sense that forced power (as Cromwell himself had realized) was less valuable than what was freely gained. 'Men conquer better', an army chaplain, Joshua Sprigge, had urged, 'as they are Saints than Soldiers'. But the word 'saints' could allude to fanatics as well as to saintly pacifists, and Cromwell had to maintain an armed power against fanaticism of Leveller and monarchist alike. In the event, he was unlikely to wield the sword for its own sake: he had dismissed an officer from the Army Council in 1647 who had remarked that no visible authority was left in the kingdom except the power of the sword. He was 'God's Englishman', to keep the spirits of the night of chaos at bay. Cromwell was in the final analysis a man who did 'both act and know'—surely high praise from a poet much preoccupied with those rival states of action and contemplation, who himself forsook 'his *Muses* dear', his Gallery, his Clora and fair singers for the 'action' of this political ode.

Yet the final word has to be suitably sceptical. Within a year of writing the ode Marvell had taken up a position in the Fairfax household. Now Fairfax had resigned his post as General of the Army on 25 July 1650 and retired to Yorkshire because he did not approve of the invasion of

Scotland. As a Presbyterian, Fairfax argued that it went against the Solemn League and Covenant, established between the two countries in 1643. Moreover, he simply did not believe that the Scots intended to invade England on Charles II's behalf. And he was correct. His political assessment, in fact, coincided with Marvell's muted critique of excessive power. Was it, perhaps, a sight of the unpublished ode that prompted Fairfax to appoint Marvell as the tutor to his daughter, Mary? Did they at least, in the Yorkshire retreat, discuss the politics and poetics of the poem?

6 Paradice's only Map

Nun Appleton House stands beside the River Wharfe a few miles to the south-east of the modern Tadcaster–York road. In a nineteenth-century *Life of the Great Lord Fairfax* (1870), the author, C.R. Markham, tells us that it consisted of a central block from which two wings stretched out to form a square open towards the river: 'the great hall or gallery occupied the centre between the two wings. It was fifty yards long... the central part of the house was surmounted by a cupola... A noble park with splendid oak-trees, and containing 300 head of deer, stretched away to the north, while on the south side were the ruins of the old Nunnery, the flower-garden, and the low meadows called *ings* extending to the banks of the Wharfe' (p.365). It is presumably this house that Markham describes

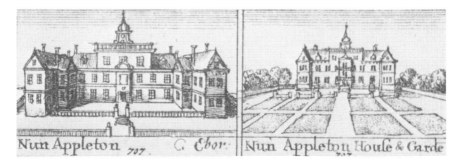

32   Nun Appleton House and Garden, two engraved views by Daniel King.

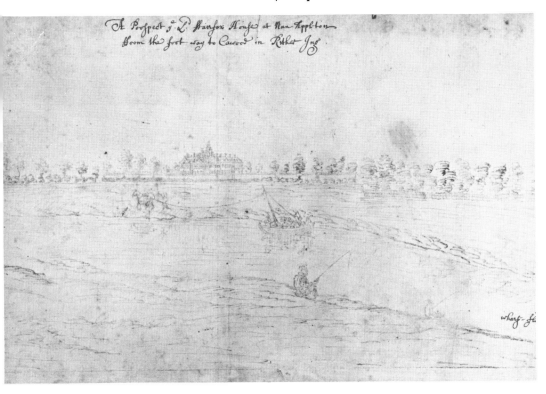

33 View of River Wharfe and Nun Appleton, drawing by William Lodge, 1670s (?).

which is recorded in two vignettes engraved by Daniel King (plate 32).
The building was reduced in size in 1712 and still partly exists today: it can
be seen to advantage from the far side of the river, where from the
churchyard at Ryther one looks across a field and over the winding river
('Among these Meads the only Snake') to a handsome building still backed
with trees. Its situation, slightly elevated above the water meadows, is
nicely captured by William Lodge's drawing, probably of the 1670s (plate
33), on which the artist has carefully recorded the name of the river and
that the 'Prospect of ye Ld. Fairfax House at Nun Appleton' was taken
from 'the foot way to Cawood in Rither Ing'. Marvell was also to attend
carefully to topographical details in his poems on Yorkshire themes, even
as he transformed them into the imagery of a far less local language.

However the house that Markham and King show us is *not* that in which
Marvell actually stayed. Markham says it was built between 1637 and 1650
(the year prior to Marvell's joining the Fairfaxes); but this information is
undocumented, though for his description of the house he relied upon
the 1711 and 1712 *Diary* of the Leeds antiquary, Ralph Thoresby, the son

of one of Fairfax's military colleagues and the inheritor of part of his collection. It is also argued that the house of Markham's and King's images could not stylistically have been completed before Fairfax's retirement in 1650: 'What remains today of the original fabric, especially the giant brick columns forming a frontispiece to the porch on the garden side and the scrolled window-surround above the main entrance, looks like London-based, not local work of the 1650s or 1660s'[46]. Moreover, if this were the building to which Marvell refers at the start of his poem, 'Upon Appleton House, to my Lord Fairfax', he is being wretchedly sycophantic: for the poem celebrates a humble dwelling without any architectural pretensions—

> Within this sober Frame expect
> Work of no Forrain *Architect*
> . . .
> *Humility* alone designs
> Those short but admirable Lines
> . . .
> A stately *Frontispice* of *Poor*
> Adorns without the open Door:
> Nor less the Rooms within commends
> Daily new *Furniture* of *Friends*.
> The House was built upon the Place
> Only as for *a Mark of Grace*;
> And for an *Inn* to entertain
> Its *Lord* a while, but not remain.

It is usually assumed that Marvell alludes there to one of Fairfax's own poems, 'Upon the New-built House at Apleton':

> Thinke not o Man that dwells herein
> This House's a stay but as an Inne
> Wch for Convenience fittly stands
> In way to one nott made wth hands. . .

And that would mean the house was newly built upon Marvell's arrival. But Fairfax could just as easily be alluding to Marvell's poem, conscientiously defending his new and grander house against the former tutor's celebration of its more modest predecessor. Very little, if anything, in Marvell's opening stanzas depends upon the completion of the new house. It is sometimes thought that Markham's 'cupola' must be referred to in the lines, 'But where he comes the swelling Hall/Stirs, and the *Square* grows *Spherical*'; but the 'cupola' seems anyway to be a rectangular lantern surmounted by an onion-like spire in both Lodge's and King's views; and Marvell may simply be continuing the images of the previous stanza and mocking students of Renaissance treatises who 'vainly strive t'immure/ The *Circle* in the *Quadrature*'.

An elderly informant of Thoresby's in 1712 remembered the 'chapel and some remains of the nunnery; saw the old house pulled down' *before* Lord Fairfax built his new one. The best suggestion is therefore that when Marvell travelled to Yorkshire the Fairfaxes were still living 'in a modest house cobbled up out of part of the nunnery'. That would sort well with his panegyric and give extra point to other lines, like

> In which we the Dimensions find
> Of that more sober Age and Mind,
> When larger sized Men did stoop
> To enter at a narrow loop;
> As practising, in doors so strait,
> To strain themselves through *Heavens Gate.*

And 'These sacred Places.../By *Vere* and *Fairfax* trod before' would acquire 'a pointed double meaning, sanctified as well as consecrated'. Finally, the Fairfaxes still living in a small house fashioned out of the 'Quarries' of the 'Neighbour-Ruine' makes much more sense of Marvell's allusion to their other homes: 'Him *Bishops-Hill,* or *Denton* may,/Or *Bilbrough,* better hold then they'.

Bishop Hill was the Fairfax house inside the city walls of York, and it was there that Marvell's pupil, Mary, was born. A less happy association must have been that during the siege of York in 1644 the General could see its roof from his position outside with the besieging parliamentary forces (Markham, p.145). He must have been positioned somewhere on the ground to the right of William Lodge's prospect of the city (plate 34), for Bishop Hill was inside and to the right of Micklegate Bar, which is the gateway visible above the roof of the hospital beside the roadway. This is the road that leads southwards from York towards Tadcaster, therefore the familiar route from Nun Appleton which we may presume Marvell would have travelled, thus seeing York for the first time much as Lodge presents it in the engraving.

The home at Denton was, in fact, the major seat, home of the 1st Lord Fairfax of Cameron. His son, who survived him by only eight years, died in 1648, so that the 3rd Lord, Marvell's employer, would have had a choice of residences when he came back to Yorkshire in 1650. That he chose Nun Appleton House, apparently his favourite, as opposed to Denton is the basis of Marvell's conceit in stanza LIX of the long poem:

> Then, to conclude these pleasant Acts,
> Denton sets ope its *Cataracts*;
> And makes the Meadow truly be
> (What it but seem'd before) a Sea.
> For, jealous of its *Lords* long stay,
> It try's t'invite him thus away.

The Cathedral of St Peter

The River Wharfe flows near enough to Denton in the West Riding to allow the conceit, but the haziness of the geography to sustain it equally suggests that Marvell was probably relying only upon family hearsay; for elsewhere he attends more punctiliously to topography.

The last of the Fairfax houses was much nearer Nun Appleton, lying just the other side of the Tadcaster–York road already mentioned. Nothing remains of the house, but the 'Hill and Grove at Bill-borow', upon which Marvell composed both English and Latin verses [pp.60–2 and 59], can still be seen from the dual carriageway; though reduced in height by subsequent gravel quarrying from the 'arched Earth' of Marvell's day, it still allows the poet's parabolic courtesy:

> See what a soft access and wide
> Lyes open to its grassy side;
> Nor with the rugged path deterrs
> The feet of breathless Travellers.

34 Prospect of York from the south-west, engraving by William Lodge.

See then how courteous it ascends,
And all the way it rises bends;
Nor for it self the height does gain,
But only strives to raise the Plain.

Maybe when it was somewhat higher, it did serve as a landmark for sailors
bringing their boats up-river towards York:

How glad the weary Seamen hast
When they salute it from the Mast!
By Night the Northern Star their way
Directs, and this no less by Day.

Marvell makes it, too, the beacon to guide Fairfax back to his native scenes (and—though Marvell was not to know—to his final resting place, alongside his wife, in Bilbrough Church). The grove, a 'Plump of aged Trees' waving upon the hilltop, is emblemized by the poet, yet at times with a delicate hesitancy ('something alwaies did appear/ Of the *great Masters* terrour there'), as if unwilling to desert its actual and natural presence or to imply what the trees themselves had been apt to learn ('ere he well the Barks could part/'Twas writ already in their Heart'). Under the poet's guidance, the grove declares, with characteristic Marvellian doubleness, its readiness to mirror both Fairfax's military acts and his contemplative retreat:

> Much other Groves, say they, then these
> And other Hills him once did please.
> Through Groves of Pikes he thunder'd then,
> And Mountains rais'd of dying Men.
> For all the *Civick Garlands* due
> To him our Branches are but few.
> Nor are our Truncks enow to bear
> The *Trophees* of one fertile Year.
>
> 'Tis true, yee Trees nor ever spoke
> More certain *Oracles* in Oak.
> But Peace (if you his favour prize)
> That Courage its own Praises flies.
> Therefore to your obscurer Seats
> From his own Brightness he retreats:
> Nor he the Hills without the Groves,
> Nor Height but with Retirement loves.

The *genius loci* and the varied genius of its proprietor delightedly coexist.

The return to Yorkshire of Thomas Fairfax was the reverse of Cromwell's progress in the 'Horatian Ode'. The corslet is now rehung upon the wall, and the 'employments' and 'recreations of my solitude' exchanged for a military career, which had been, until then, his whole life and fame (plate 35—notice the 'groves of pikes' beyond the General's prancing horse). It is his military fame and skill that Milton praised in a sonnet 'To my Lord Fairfax', just before the King's execution:

> Fairfax, whose Name in Arms through *Europe* rings,
> And fills all Mouths with Envy or with Praise,
> And all her Jealous Monarchs with Amaze.
> And Rumours loud which daunt remotest Kings,
> Thy firm unshaken Valour ever brings
> Victory home, while new Rebellions raise
> Their Hydra-heads, and the false *North* displays
> Her broken League to Imp her Serpent Wings...

86

His
Excellencie
Sr Thomas Fairfax Kt
Generall of the forces
raised by tee
Parliament

Printed for John Partridg . Edua Bowers Pinxit

35　Thomas Fairfax, engraved portrait by William Marshall after painting by Edward Bower, 1647.

Milton's reservations at that time seem to coincide with Marvell's 'Ode' and with the General's own worries about unnecessary power levelled against either King or Scots, and the sestet voices ambitions larger than the mere victories of civil war:

> O yet! a Nobler task awaits thy Hand,
> > For what can War, but Acts of War still breed,
> > Till injur'd Truth from Violence be freed;
> > And publick Faith be rescu'd from the Brand
> > Of publick Fraud; in vain doth Valour bleed,
> > While Avarice and Rapine shares the Land.

Some similar distress at political events finally drove Fairfax to Yorkshire. His wife, who also came from a military family, the Veres, and who had spent much of her life among soldiers and on manoeuvres, must have advocated this retirement even more strongly than her husband. An avid Presbyterian, she hated Cromwell and the Independents; she had also made a determined stand against arbitrary government, having urged violent means to save the King from execution. From their Yorkshire retirement Fairfax maintained, without secrecy, a correspondence with Charles II and headed the deputation for his return in 1660.

Fairfax was only thirty-eight when he came to Yorkshire in 1650, but he needed the refreshments and recuperations that the country offered. Here he resumed rural pursuits (he wrote about horse breeding) and attended to his cabinet of curiosities and collection of coins, medals, engravings, manuscripts and books. Most of these passed eventually to Ralph Thoresby, whose father had served with the General, and items from Fairfax's collection are identified in Thoresby's catalogue of his *musaeum*, reprinted in *Ducatus Leodiensis* (1715). Besides horse breeding and his collections, Fairfax wrote church history, translated poetry, and wrote his own. It must, in short, have been a highly congenial ambience for Andrew Marvell, and it is perhaps easy to understand his enthusiastic celebration of Fairfax's estate in 'Upon Appleton House, to my Lord Fairfax' [pp.62–86].

A manuscript of Fairfax's survives in the Bodleian Library at Oxford, duly divided into religious 'employments' and secular 'recreations'. The first entry under the second heading is a translation or 'imitation' of the French poet's, Saint-Amant's, 'La Solitude' (plate 36):

> O how I love these Solitudes
> And places silent as the Night
> Ther where noe thronging multituds
> Disturbe wth noyse ther sweet delight
> O how myn eyes are pleas'd to see
> Oakes that such spreadinge branches beare

552

The Solitude

O how I love these solitudes
And places silent as the night
Ther wher noe thronging multituds
Dis turbe wth noyse ther swet delight
O how myn eyes are pleas'd to see
Okes that such spreading branches beare
Wch from old time's nativity
And th'enuy of so many yeares
Ar still greene Beautifull & faire
As all the world's first day they were

Naught but the highest twiggs of all
wher zephyrus doth wanton play

36 'The Solitude', manuscript poem by Thomas Fairfax.

> Wch from old Time's netiuity
> And th'envy of so many yeares
> Are still greene beautifull & faire
> As att the world's first day they were.

There is no knowing when these verses were composed, but one suspects that they must date from *after* Marvell's stay at Nun Appleton. So that the various echoes of 'The Solitude' that one hears in Marvell's various Yorkshire poems[47] must, in all likelihood, be the General's debts to his temporary poet in residence. It is a pleasant thought that, besides giving 'some instructions in the languages to the lady, his daughter' (Milton to Bradshaw), Marvell's own writings taught the General ways of looking at and describing the landscape of his retirement. 'The genius of my Rural Muse' recalls Marvell's conceit of the River Wharfe—'Among these Meads the only Snake'—and translates it (rather flatly) into the simile of the stream 'glidinge under th'arbored banks/As windinge Serpents in the grass'. Marvell's river, again,

> in what wanton harmless folds
> It ev'ry where the Meadow holds;
> And its yet muddy back doth lick,
> Till as a *Chrystal Mirrour* slick;
> Where all things gaze themselves, and doubt
> If they be in it or without.

flows more muddily in Fairfax's

> Sometimes soe Cleare & soe serene
> Itt seemes ast were a looking glass
> And to our Vewes presenting seemes
> As heavens beneath the waters was
> The Sun in it's soe clearely seemes
> That contemplatinge this bright sight
> As't was a doubt whether itt had beene
> Himselfe or image gave the light
> Att first appearing to our eyes
> As if he had falne from the skyes.

Nor is it improbable (though dates are uncertain) to trace the lineage of Fairfax's couplet—'Times past Fawnes Satyrs Demy-Gods/Hither retird to seeke for Aide'—back to the Mower's confidence in his attack on gardens that 'The Gods themselves with us do dwell' in the *meadows*. Imitation is, of course, a mode of flattery, and it is good that Fairfax could return some compliments.

'Upon Appleton House', long out of favour with readers, has recently attracted much attention, at least from the critics. It certainly deserves it from all readers. This long meditation upon the Yorkshire estate where he found himself in the early 1650s is Marvell's most original and exciting composition. This achievement derives partly from its inclusiveness—the poem touches upon almost all of the concerns of the poet's life to that point, as well as looking ahead, and of the age he lived in—and partly from the skill with which all these materials are controlled: 'all things are composed here' (IV.25)*; as in the garden, so in the poem. It glances at Fairfax's career, at political and social issues (the Levellers, for instance), at rival types of existence both as they concerned Fairfax and as they touched the poet's own position; it revives old Renaissance debates between art and nature in the experienced context of an actual estate.

The inclusiveness, which is one of the major achievements in 'Upon Appleton House', is, I suspect, endemic to the seventeenth-century garden. As a poet, Marvell would be characteristically attentive to the classical literature of villas and country estates (for detailed accounts of these literary models see the critical works cited in notes 47 and 55). But, as we have seen with visitors to Italy, modern Renaissance villas and gardens often seemed to realize those written accounts of the classical past in visible and usable shape. So that literary traditions were included in the meanings of or responses to an Italianate garden, just as they are at Nun Appleton. Further, the gardens Marvell would have seen abroad (above, chapter 4) were themselves veritable compendia of idea and image. Not for nothing did visitors praise their variety or what Evelyn called a 'Theatre for Pastimes' (p.393). Theatre, in this usage, means a collection, and European gardens, besides being shaped like theatres and sometimes containing theatres, offered a whole abstract of the world outside. Milton, perhaps recalling the paradises he had once seen for himself in Italy, talks in *Paradise Lost* (IV.206-7) of the Garden of Eden as offering 'To all delight of human sense exposed/In narrow room nature's whole wealth'. A similar claim for the inclusiveness of Nun Appleton is put forward by Marvell himself at the end of his poem—

> 'Tis not, what once it was, the *World*;
> But a rude heap together hurl'd;
> All negligently overthrown,
> Gulfes, Deserts, Precipices, Stone.
> Your lesser *World* contains the same.
> But in more decent Order tame;
> *You Heaven's Center, Nature's Lap.*
> *And Paradise's only Map.* (XCVI. 761-8)

Nun Appleton could not, of course, have been anything like the gardens of modern Europe; yet Marvell seems to look at and to 'read' its capabilities with a modish and travelled eye (European sights are often on his mind during the poem). And it comes as no surprise to think of his doing so, for one of his fundamental poetic strategies is to apply to an old-fashioned idea a structure of other, more up-to-date ideas (and vice versa).

The European Renaissance garden presented, we have seen, imagery

---

*Since it is a long poem and readers may wish to locate quotations in other texts, I give stanza, followed by line, numbers.

37 *The Villa D'Este at Tivoli*, artist unknown, seventeenth century.

for the visitor to read. At Nun Appleton, the ruined nunnery, the present
living accommodation of the Fairfaxes and the General's flower garden
announced national and familial history and philosophical ideas. The
poet's scrutiny of these 'messages' is along the same lines as Evelyn's
viewing Rubens's 'history of the late tumults' at the Cour in Brussels
(above, pp.36–7) or those innumerable visitors to the Villa D'Este (plate
37), deciphering from statues, fountains and inscriptions a whole

panegyric of the Estes and the town of Tivoli which their pleasure house graced. Marvell even alludes directly to this sort of visit to palaces and gardens, along with a recollection of his Roman visit:

> And surely when the after Age
> Shall hither come in *Pilgrimage,*
> These sacred Places to adore,
> By *Vere* and *Fairfax* trod before,
> Men will dispute how their Extent
> Within such dwarfish Confines went:

And some will smile at this, as well
As *Romulus* his Bee-like Cell.   (V.33–40)

The house and gardens, then, if properly understood, declare the man
and his family. The Renaissance presented these histories in much
elaborate symbolism, whereas in Roman times, as the younger Pliny
wrote[48], it was often a question of spelling out the owner's name in topiary
work. (Marvell may well have in mind Pliny's descriptions of villas and
gardens, for his lines on draughts in 'hollow Palaces... Where Winds as
he themselves may lose' (III.19–20) take up another of Pliny's concerns).
Fairfax's house, at least, seems to emulate that Roman *simplicitas*, and we
notice how the architectural fabric is deemed to be the plastic expression
of his moral qualities:

> *Humility* alone designs
> Those short but admirable Lines,
> By which, ungirt and unconstrain'd,
> Things greater are in less contain'd.   (VI.41–4)

> So Honour better Lowness bears.
> Then That unwonted Greatness wears.
> Height with a certain Grace does bend,
> But low Things clownishly ascend.
> And yet what needs there here Excuse,
> Where ev'ry Thing does answer Use?
> Where neatness nothing can condemn,
> Nor Pride invent what to contemn?   (VIII.57–64)

(Alexander Pope was later to make a similar claim in his *Epistle to
Burlington:* 'You show us, Rome was glorious, not profuse,/And pompous
buildings once were things of Use'). So if Marvell is keeping in mind at
Nun Appleton his Italian experience of gardens, this does not mean (with
a *snobisme de voyage*) that he loses his instinct for due tact and indigenous
style, his confidence in people before property or upholstery:

> A Stately *Frontispice* of *Poor*
> Adorns without the open Door:
> Nor less the Rooms within commends
> Daily new *Furniture* of *Friends*.   (IX.65–8)

The imagery of *frontispiece*, which could mean both architectural facade
and the first page of a book, seventeenth-century examples of which
could often invoke elaborate symbolism and usually included some
architectural device—further supports the poet's concern to *read* the
contents of house and garden.

In all gardens man's art coexists and mingles with natural elements. At Nun Appleton

> Nature here hath been so free
> As if she said leave this to me.
> Art would more neatly have defac'd
> What she had laid so sweetly wast;
> In fragrant Gardens, shaddy Woods,
> Deep Meadows, and transparent Floods.   (X.75–80)

Marvell certainly sees the whole estate, as he saw the living accommodation, as unpretentious, 'natural' and an apt expression of the proprietor, celebrated in another poem as teaching the Bilbrough trees to grow 'so streight and green'. But as his own poetic art shapes the elements of its material, so the Fairfax demesne is obviously not a simple matter of natural accident; positioning and disposition of house, old nunnery, garden and park *vis-à-vis* the river and the rest of the wooded estate are questions of human decision and design. What Marvell obviously delights to do in his garden poetry is explore at any one appropriate moment the paradoxical tensions of the art-nature dialogue, stressing as he does at this point of the Nun Appleton poem, one of the extremer positions. Similarly, 'The Mower against Gardens' [pp.43–4], partly because its speaker is a figure of meadow not lawn (though how else but by mowers were grassy areas within gardens kept trimmed?), explores the 'naturalistic' argument:

> Luxurious Man, to bring his Vice in use,
>   Did after him the World seduce:
> And from the fields the Flow'rs and Plants allure,
>   Where Nature was most plain and pure.
> He first enclos'd within the Gardens square
>   A dead and standing pool of Air
>   . . .
> 'Tis all enforc'd: the Fountain and the Grot;
>   While the sweet Fields do lye forgot:
> Where willing Nature does to all dispence
>   A wild and fragrant Innocence...

Other Mower poems generously link the speaker to his natural world:

> I am the Mower *Damon,* known
> Through all the Meadows I have mown.
> On me the Morn her dew distills
> Before her darling Daffadils.
> And, if at Noon my toil me heat,
> The Sun himself licks off my Sweat.
> While, going home, the Ev'ning sweet
> In cowslip-water bathes my feet.   [p.46]

And in 'The Mower to the Glo-Worms' the light of the worms provides both nightingale and countryman with illumination (Evelyn captured 'flying *Glow-wormes* cald Luccioli' (p.427) to read by on the boat from Bologna to Ferrara; so Marvell's conceit, as I suspect is often the case, keeps its eye firmly upon actualities). But man's active *use* of natural events—as the Mower himself claims in those last two examples—constitutes an art, the art of blending his skills with the natural potential of a scene. It becomes, as Marvell proceeds through the Nun Appleton estate, a covert analogy for that other necessary fusion of action and contemplation, involvement with man's world and retirement into nature's.

The initial survey of the 'fragrant Gardens, shaddy Woods,/Deep Meadows, and transparent Floods' takes in their various delights with 'slow Eyes' before the visitors 'on each pleasant footstep stay' (XI.11–12). This 'overview' is a peculiarly Italian experience: since so many gardens in that country are constructed on sloping sites—the Villa D'Este, for example (plate 37)—the visitor could overlook the whole 'Theatre for Pastimes' before descending to examine every section. This Italian experience is admirably epitomized by Henry Wotton in his *Elements of Architecture:*

I have seene a *Garden* (for the maner perchance incomparable) into which the first Accesse was a high walke like a Tarrace, from whence might bee taken a generall view of the whole *Plott* below but rather in a delightfull confusion, then with any plaine distinction of the pieces. From this the *Beholder* descending many steps, was afterwards conveyed againe, by severall *mountings* and *valings,* to various entertainements of his *sent,* and *sight:* which I shall not neede to describe (for that were poeticall) let me onely note this, that every one of these diversities, was as if hee had beene Magically transported into a new Garden.   (pp.109–10)

Now Nun Appleton was on no such sloping site, but the poet's elevation above his material allows him the same perspective. Characteristically, Marvell enjoys his large 'Generall view', as he also responds to the magical transformations of scene later in the meadows.

He comes first to the ruined nunnery. Like Sandys among the classical ruins of the Bay of Naples (above p.47), he traces the history that still fills their vacancies:

> We opportunly may relate
> The Progress of this Houses Fate.
> A *Nunnery* first gave it birth.
> For *Virgin Buildings* oft brought forth.
> And all that Neighbour-Ruine shows
> The Quarries whence this dwelling rose.   (XI.83–8)

The story that unfolds has often been considered too lengthy, too disproportionate in the poem as a whole. On two counts, this is surely wrong. First, as we have seen[49], visits to palaces, country houses and their gardens frequently initiated long meditations upon past, present and even future:

> Is not this he whose Offspring fierce
> Shall fight through all the *Universe*;
> And with successive Valour try
> *France, Poland*, either *Germany*;
> Till one, as long since prophecy'd,
> His Horse through conquer'd *Britain* ride?
> Yet, against Fate, his Spouse they kept;
> And the great Race would intercept.   (XXXI.241-8)

The actual architecture that we see (in this case, the ruin) leads us on by emblem or symbol (coats of arms, for instance), or simply by being itself and demanding our understanding, to appreciate its fuller significance. But there is, Marvell realizes (perhaps more than do the Fairfaxes themselves), a more complex meaning to this ruined nunnery. Second, the nunnery and the tale of the prioress who tried to coerce Isabel Thwaites early in the sixteenth century promote reflection upon the two themes that are absolutely central to the Nun Appleton milieu: that of the proper occasion and uses of retreat or retirement; that of the rival roles of art and nature.

A ruined monastery or nunnery would declare, especially to such a staunchly Protestant family as the Fairfaxes, the whole historical basis of their freedom from Roman Catholicism. As tutor in such a family, Marvell makes the idea of a cloistered religion ridiculous, even pernicious. Its artificiality dishonours its natural location (see stanza X), and the 'Arts' of the nuns, the full and free expression of a human life. Marvell wittily makes the prioress aware that their arts of embroidery cannot manage to express everything—'"But what the Linnen can't receive/They in their Lives do interweave"' (XVI.125-6). But, more insidiously, she is given speeches that recall to any person in the 1650s some issues (Liberty, fighting, succession) which, so the implication must be, simply cannot be resolved by retreat into the unstrenuous existence of a nunnery:

> 'Within this holy leisure we
> 'Live innocently as you see.

[the verse there is appropriately inert]

> 'These Walls restrain the World without,
> 'But hedge our Liberty about.

> 'These Bars inclose that wider Den
> 'Of those wild Creatures, called Men.
> 'The Cloyster outward shuts its Gates,
> 'And, from us, locks on them the Grates.
>
> 'Here we, in shining Armour white,
> 'Like *Virgin Amazons* do fight...'   (XIII–XIV.97–106)

It is the effortless ease which Isabel Thwaites is promised—'The Rule itself to you shall bend' or 'How soft the yoke' (XX.156 and 159)—and which is so transparently at odds with the spiritual regimen of current Protestantism that declares its insufficiency. Isabel Thwaites might model the Virgin for the embroidering nuns, but her proposed retreat offers no further scope for us to imitate, whatever the prioress argues:

> 'And your Example, if our Head,
> 'Will soon us to perfection lead.
> 'Those Virtues to us all so dear,
> 'Will straight grow Sanctity when here:
> 'And that, once sprung, increase so fast
> 'Till Miracles it work at last...'   (XXI.163–8)

As the great-great-grandmother of Marvell's patron, she is appropriately rescued; but not before the earlier Fairfax has been confronted with the same moral and political dilemmas as his seventeenth-century descendant:

> What should he do? He would respect
> Religion, but not Right neglect:
> For first Religion taught him Right,
> And dazled not but clear'd his sight.
> Sometimes resolv'd his Sword he draws,
> But reverenceth then the Laws:
> For Justice still that Courage led;
> First from a Judge, then Souldier bred.   (XXIX.225–32)

The siege and storming of the nunnery (stanza XXXII) amusingly plays with the imagery of Fairfax's military career and leads smoothly on to Marvell's consideration of what a general, as opposed to a nun, does in retreat.

But the section on the cloistered life of the nuns also glances at Fairfax himself. True, the building was 'no Religious House till now', when the Fairfaxes have properly made it one. But the poet, ever quick to note alternative states, seems aware of the disadvantages of retreat. He can suggest scepticisms, too, without damaging the surface texture of the homage; indeed, to imply that Fairfax's retirement is a less than adequate

realization of his potential is simply to compliment him and lament his
inactivity in England's cause. In Marvell's consideration of the General's
flower garden and of his own situation at the end of the poem we shall see
that he finds problems as well as compensations in withdrawal. Such
suggestions are mooted first when, with him, we look at and 'read' the
nunnery buildings.

The transition from nunnery to garden and, accordingly, from history
to present concerns, is managed with that magical progression which
Wotton experienced in Italian gardens:

> From that blest Bed the *Heroe* came,
> Whom *France* and *Poland* yet does fame:
> Who, when retired here to Peace,
> His warlike Studies could not cease;
> But laid these Gardens out in sport
> In the just Figure of a Fort;
> And with five Bastions it did fence,
> As aiming one for ev'ry Sense.   (XXXVI.281–8)

The poet moves from the ruins into the garden fort and his mind glides
from one consideration to another. The extended conceit which follows
must have flattered and delighted General Fairfax, as it can us:

> When in the *East* the Morning Ray
> Hangs out the Colours of the Day,
> The Bee through these known Allies hums,
> Beating the *Dian* with its *Drumms.*   [Dian = reveille]
> Then Flow'rs their drowsie Eylids raise,
> Their Silken Ensigns each displayes,
> And dries its Pan yet dank with Dew,
> And fills its Flask with Odours new.
>
> These, as their *Governour* goes by,
> In fragrant Vollyes they let fly;
> And to salute their *Governess*
> Again as great a charge they press:
> None for the *Virgin Nymph*; for She
> Seems with the Flow'rs a Flow'r to be.
> And think so still! though not compare
> With Breath so sweet, or Cheek so faire.
>
> Well shot ye Firemen! Oh how sweet,
> And round your equal Fires do meet;
> Whose shrill report no Ear can tell,
> But Ecchoes to the Eye and smell.
> See how the Flow'rs as at *Parade*,
> Under their *Colours* stand displaid:

Each *Regiment* in order grows,
That of the Tulip Pinke and Rose.

But when the vigilant *Patroul*
Of Stars walks round about the *Pole*,
Their Leaves, that to the stalks are curl'd,
Seem to their Staves the *Ensigns* furl'd.
Then in some Flow'rs beloved Hut
Each Bee as Sentinel is shut;
And sleeps so too: but, if once stir'd,
She runs you through, or askes *the Word*.   (XXXVII–XL.289–320)

Yet perhaps we are also, without disproportion, meant to be struck by the slight silliness of it all. Gardens could in practice have been just as contrived—we may recall the military imagery which Brereton found near The Hague (above, p.44)—and Marvell matches it with an equivalent verbal conceit. But the poet who invented the Mower was also ready to scoff at absurd 'enforcements' either of garden art or of personality. Fairfax's Yorkshire pursuits only mimic his earlier career, and it is strongly hinted in one stanza how much England has lost by the General's decision to absolve himself from current events, notably from the Council of State, where he shared with his fellow members the offices of Warden of the Cinque Ports and Lord High Admiral[50]:

And yet their walks one on the Sod
Who, had it pleased him and *God*,
Might once have made our Gardens spring
Fresh as his own and flourishing.
But he preferr'd to the *Cinque Ports*
These five imaginary Forts:
And, in those half-dry Trenches, spann'd
Pow'r which the Ocean might command.   (XLIV.345–52)

Marvell at once explains that Fairfax put his *conscience* before his *ambition* at the time of the proposed Scottish expedition. But the hint is nevertheless sown of a less than total realization of the man's potential. And the poet has at the very least initiated the process by which he comes to feel that Nun Appleton cannot detain him either from the larger world of activism outside.

In stanza XLI Marvell had sounded for the first time the theme of Nun Appleton as metonym for England. But it stands for an England before it was destroyed by civil wars. Such an image of a lost garden further involves the idea of Nun Appleton as Paradise, an Edenic world where 'The *Gardiner* had the *Souldiers* place' and 'The Nursery of all things green/Was then the only *Magazeen*' (XLIII.337–40):

100

38   Water meadows at Nun Appleton.

> Oh Thou, that dear and happy Isle
> The Garden of the World ere while,
> Thou *Paradise* of four Seas,
> Which *Heaven* planted us to please,
> But, to exclude the World, did guard
> With watry if not flaming Sword;
> What luckless Apple did we tast,
> To make us Mortal, and the Wast?   (XLI.321–8)

Fairfax's retreat at Nun Appleton (did Marvell relish the pun in *Nun Apple*ton?) has recovered, as effectively as mortals can, that unfallen world of paradise and England. This reconstitution of that golden world in Marvell's poem as in Fairfax's estate is paralleled locally by the modern dwelling rising out of the ruins of the nunnery and, further away, as a memory of Europe, those modern villas emulating and even created within their classical predecessors (plate 18).

With the larger relevance of this Yorkshire scene now established, at least in outline, Marvell moves into 'the Abbyss. . . Of that unfathomable Grass'; the remainder of the poem takes place in the water meadows or ings and woods of the estate. Although the gardens at Nun Appleton no longer help us with Marvell's poem, their relationship with the meadows and woods and the general topography of the area are still relevant. Plate

39   Villa Lante, Bagnaia, woodcut from *Descrizione di Roma Moderna*, 1697.

38 is a view from the bottom of the present garden eastwards along the
natural 'ha-ha' or dyke dividing the grounds from the water meadows,
which can be seen as a flat expanse stretching towards the river out of
sight on the right. The elevation of Nun Appleton grounds above these
fields was probably deliberate, to ensure that the river's flood waters did

not invade the gardens. This topography is what the poem alludes to in stanza XLVII, when Marvell announces his descent from the gardens into the lower and larger area of the estate.

What is crucial to understand here is that in leaving the 'formal' garden Marvell does not leave behind habits of mind appropriate to that area. Once again Italy provides the analogy and, I imagine, the example: its gardens often existed in close juxtaposition to groves or other irregular naturalistic areas, into which the imagery and symbolism were extended, although not usually in such profusion[51]. The Villa Lante at Bagnaia, for instance, had around two sides of its 'formal' terraces woodland groves in which were pavilions and fountains (including the Fountain of Pegasus, linked iconologically to the lodges of the Muses inside the main garden); this is depicted crudely but clearly in a woodcut often used in travellers' guidebooks (plate 39). When Marvell, at Nun Appleton, descends into the meadows and woods, he continues to 'read' them as he had the ruins and flower garden:

> Here in the Morning tye my Chain,
> Where the two Woods have made a Lane;
> While, like a Guard on either side,
> The Trees before their *Lord* divide;
> This, like a long and equal Thread,
> Betwixt two *Labyrinths* does lead.
> But, where the Floods did lately drown,
> There at the Ev'ning stake me down. (LXXVIII.617–24)

He 'sees' the woodland still answering Fairfax's military presence, recalling those high alleys through groves of an Italian villa, with maze-like compartments hidden behind their hedges. Three stanzas later the poet imagines himself like some river god (plate 22), 'Abandoning my lazy Side,/Stretcht as a Bank unto the Tide'. The appearance of Mary Fairfax, the studied climax of the poem, is also couched in language that would apply as well to the statues which gave meaning and significance to the parts of a garden over which they presided:

> 'Tis *She* that to these Gardens gave
> That wondrous Beauty which they have;
> *She* streightness on the Woods bestows;
> To *Her* the Meadow sweetness owes;
> Nothing could make the River be
> So Chrystal-pure but only *She*;
> *She* yet more Pure, Sweet, Streight, and Fair,
> Then Gardens, Woods, Meads, Rivers are.
>
> Therefore what first *She* on them spent,
> They gratefully again present. (LXXXVII–LXXXVIII.689–98)

The languages with which Marvell, the '*easie Philosopher*', confers 'Among the *Birds* and *Trees*' are drawn from many activities. Mary Fairfax, as well as being seen as some gardenesque presence, some statue defining *genius loci*, is also described in the literary terms of an old tradition that tells how 'all things flourished in the presence of the beloved and withered at her departure'[52]. But such literary and other philosophical traditions, it may be argued, had been translated into fact, realized and given three-dimensional substance in countless Renaissance gardens. Hence, a gardenist vocabulary not only suits a poetry about Nun Appleton, but it aids the inclusiveness which I have said is one of the poem's ambitions.

For the world of 'unfathomable Grass' Marvell draws upon the language of masque and theatre:

> No Scene that turns with Engines strange
> Does oftner then these Meadows change. (XLIX.385–6)

The elaborate transformation scenes of the old court masques and the revolving shutters of the Vitruvian theatre set the tone of wonderful changefulness in the park, where nature assists art in creating a world of delicate ambiguity:

40 Fountain mechanism, engraving from Salomon de Caus, *Les Raisons des Forces Mouvantes* (1615).

41 *Medici Villa at Pratolino*, detail of painted lunette by Giusto Utens, 1599.

> The modest *Halcyon* comes in sight,
> Flying betwixt the Day and Night;
> . . .
> And Men the silent *Scene* assist,
> Charm'd with the *Saphir-winged Mist.* (LXXXIV–LXXXV.669–80)

The '*Scene*', of which we are often reminded, is a theatrical setting, and its changes mark the progress of Nun Appleton's masque:

> This *Scene* again withdrawing brings
> A new and empty Face of things;
> A levell'd space, as smooth and plain...   (LVI.441–3)

But a magical succession of scenes is, as Wotton knew (above, p.96), as central to the experience of a garden as a masque. Gardens in Italy and France had usually contained theatres, and it was easy for the language of one art to be invoked about the other. English visitors to the Villa D'Este

105

continued to use masque vocabulary about their experiences there long after the performance of masques stopped in England in 1640. Nor was this simply hyperbolic, for hydraulic machinery could engineer extraordinary events (plate 40). Pratolino, a Medici villa north of Florence, delighted travellers with its numerous grottoes (plate 41) where they saw 'Galatea who comes out of a Dore in a Sea Chariot with two Nymphs, and saileth a while upon the Water, and so returns again in at the same Dore...the Samaritan Woman coming out of her house with her buckets to fetch water...and all this done by water, which sets these little inventions awork, and makes them move as it were of themselves'[53]. Such effects are close to the delights that Marvell both sees and invents among the woods and meadows of Yorkshire. Even the floods released from the Denton area (stanza LIX) are no more than a natural version of the flooding of the courtyard of the Pitti Palace in Florence for another, aquatic Medici entertainment.

Metamorphosis is, then, endemic to gardens and to masques. The Mower complained as much about man's botanical experiments ('The Pink grew then as double as his Mind', p.43), while 'The Garden' itself wittily explains the gods' delight in a green world as their pursuit of metamorphosis:

> The *Gods*, that mortal Beauty chase,
> Still in a Tree did end their race.
> *Apollo* hunted *Daphne* so,
> Only that She might Laurel grow.
> And *Pan* did after *Syrinx* speed,
> Not as a Nymph, but for a Reed.   [p.52]

The poetry invokes exactly the same legends of transformation as were often realized in garden devices: at the Villa Aldobrandini in Frascati there was a whole grotto filled with paintings (now in the National Gallery, London) in which Domenichino depicted the actual process of metamorphosis (plate 42). Marvell's vision of the Nun Appleton landscape affords a variety of similar pictures: men in the meadows seem changed to grasshoppers, grasshoppers to giants (stanza XLVII). In the woods 'arching Boughs' become 'Corintheon Porticoes' (stanza LXIV). By the riverside, the reflections mimic the real world to the confusion of both:

> as a *Chrystal Mirrour* slick;
> Where all things gaze themselves, and doubt
> If they be in it or without.   (LXXX.636–8)

This confusion is also explained in the language of painting, whether 'Mexique Paintings'—images created with feathers (stanza LXXIII), the

42 *Apollo Pursuing Daphne*, by Domenichino Zampieri and assistants, 1616–18.

43 Final section of 'Landscape' instructions (how 'to bequile and cozen y^e owne eyes'), from Daniel King's manuscript art treatise, formerly belonging to Mary Fairfax, 1653–7.

painting of 'Traverse' scenes in a theatre (stanza LIII), which deceive in the same fashion as painted prospects in gardens, or the painting of landscapes:

> They seem within the polisht Grass
> A Landskip drawn in Looking-Glass.   (LVIII.457–8)

Landscape paintings were generally analysed in terms of their deception of the eye—offering in two dimensions the illusion of three-dimensional space. In a manuscript treatise written for Mary Fairfax by another of her tutors, Daniel King, some time after Marvell's departure, this conventional emphasis upon the deceptions of landscape art is reiterated (plate 43)[54]. In 'The Nymph complaining', also maybe dating from this Yorkshire period, the *trompe-l'oeil*—the white fawn camouflaged among the lilies—and metamorphosis—'Had it liv'd long, it would have been/Lilies without, Roses within'—provide further examples of Marvell's fascination with the deceits and transformations of a garden world.

Given this metamorphic landscape at Nun Appleton and the tradition by which a garden declared its owner's history, it seems perfectly plausible to read allusions to contemporary politics in various passages. The whole mowing scene (stanzas L *et seq.*) has seemed, at least to one critic[55], an allegory of the Civil War; certainly by the time we come to the 'Traverse' painting of

> A Camp of Battail newly fought:
> Where, as the Meads with Hay, the Plain
> Lyes quilted ore with Bodies slain:
> The Women that with forks it fling,
> Do represent the Pillaging.   (LIII.420–4)

it is inconceivable that Marvell's patron would not see the larger events of wartime mirrored in the poem's conceits. Fairfax had had trouble with Levellers in the army before his resignation, so their mention (stanza LVII) would also glance from the poetic to the political field. Such references—others include a doubtful allusion to Charles I in the figure of the oak during the section on the woodpecker (stanzas LXVIII–LXX)—need not be taken as solemn reminders of the troubled world before or beyond Nun Appleton; they allude, with all their humorous invention, to events which the Yorkshire estate is fortunate to include only by the poet's wit. Just as the meadows dwarf the men who descend into their abyss, so Nun Appleton generally distances and diminishes the outer world's affairs.

Marvell's duties as tutor kept him, one assumes, contented. It was probably early in the years in Yorkshire that he composed lines 'To his

worthy Friend Doctor Witty upon his Translation of the Popular Errors';
Witty's book appeared in 1651 and Marvell's poem refers to a 'Caelia' in
terms that make it probable that he alludes to Mary Fairfax:

> *Caelia* whose English doth more richly flow
> Then *Tagus*, purer then dissolved snow,
> And sweet as are her lips that speak it, she
> Now learns the tongues of *France* and *Italy*;
> But she is *Caelia* still: no other grace
> But her own smiles commend that lovely face;
> Her native beauty's not Italianated,
> Nor her chast mind into the *French* translated:
> Her thoughts are *English*, though her sparkling wit
> With other Language doth them fitly fit.   [p.98]

It is a graceful compliment, echoed in the longer poem, both to his
friend's translation and to his current employer. The girl, thus
epitomized, is the appropriate goddess of the Nun Appleton park, 'where
yet She leads her studious Hours' (XCIV.746). Though Marvell glances
ahead to a worthy marriage for her—

> (Till Fate her worthily translates,
> And find a Fairfax for our Thwaites)   (XCIV.747–8)

he would not know that in 1657 she would be married to the second Duke
of Buckingham, elder brother to Francis Villiers whose death Marvell had
already mourned. Buckingham was to prove one of the worst rakes of the
age, and his wife (plate 44) certainly needed all the virtues which the poet
claimed for her before her marriage. But in the early 1650s the world
beyond Nun Appleton, still unknown to Marvell as to his pupil herself,
cannot threaten the '*Domestick Heaven*' in which Mary is nursed. The
poet's panegyric identifies her closely with the natural world in which they
are both involved: if she rises above it, the higher world is consonant with
the parkland, not a Yorkshire Babel:

> The Meadow Carpets where to tread;
> The Garden Flow'rs to Crown *Her* Head;
> And for a Glass the limpid Brook,
> Where *She* may all *her* Beautyes look;
> But, since *She* would not have them seen,
> The Wood about *her* draws a Skreen.
>
> For *She*, to higher Beauties rais'd,
> Disdains to be for lesser prais'd.
> *She* counts her Beauty to converse
> In all the Languages as *hers*,
> Nor yet in those *her self* imploves

44   *Mary (Fairfax), Countess of Buckingham,* artist unknown.

> But for the *Wisdome,* not the *Noyse;*
> Nor yet that *Wisdome* would affect,
> But as 'tis *Heavens Dialect.*   (LXXXVIII–LXXXIX.699–712)

'Heavens Dialect', as we have seen, is a language which Nun Appleton itself speaks and teaches to its poet, himself a teacher of languages. It is a Paradise, an Eden, where even rotten oaks, reminding us of human error

111

with sly glances at the serpent of the Fall, can still be absorbed into a beneficent pattern:

> Nor would it, had the Tree not fed
> A *Traitor-worm,* within it bred.
> (As first our *Flesh* corrupt within
> Tempts impotent and bashful *Sin.*)
> And yet that *Worm* triumphs not long,
> But serves to feed the *Hewels young.*
> While the Oake seems to fall content,
> Viewing the Treason's Punishment.   (LXX.553–60)

It is, like that other fall in 'The Garden'—'Insnar'd with Flow'rs, I fall on Grass'—essentially an innocent occurrence. Yet any mention of Paradise necessarily implies man's expulsion from it; of innocence, experience; of the royal oak, its treasonous self-corruption and punishment. 'The Garden' had also obliquely reminded us that man did not stay in the first Eden:

> Two Paradises 'twere in one
> To live in Paradise alone.

So perhaps we may play with Marvell's meaning (he is himself playing with the idea of a 'happy Garden-state. . . without a mate') and read that couplet as a recognition that simply to exist in that Yorkshire Paradise and *no where else* would be both a double felicity and a double jeopardy. Marvell certainly pleads in stanza LXXVII 'never to leave this Place'; but inasmuch as Nun Appleton is 'Paradice's only Map', his banishment from it is inevitable. Why he left the Fairfaxes' employment we do not know. In a reference to their child, Marvell's pupil, the parents are said in the poem to 'make their *Destiny* their *Choice*'. So ironically did Adam; so perhaps deliberately did Marvell. Choosing to leave and make his career in the political world of London, from which, his poem implies so often, Nun Appleton is far removed, is to opt freely for what would eventually be necessitated. It is also totally characteristic of Marvell's fascination for antithetical states that having fully appreciated the values of retreat, solitude and contemplation he wants to try involvement, business and activism. Nor can he, aged thirty-two, stay for ever as a teacher of languages.

> The Forward Youth that would appear
> Must now forsake his *Muses* dear,
> Nor in the Shadows sing
> His Numbers languishing.

7 Your Excellencyes most humble and faithfull Servant

Political service may have been Marvell's aim in returning to London; but he found himself, at least for a while, a tutor once again, this time to a protégé of Oliver Cromwell's. The details of this sequence of events are only partly clear. We may assume that he left Yorkshire about the end of 1652; that would allow enough time for him to have got into contact with Milton (plate 45), from whom he solicited support in his political career and who, accordingly, is found writing to John Bradshaw, Lord-President of the Council of State, on 21 February 1653 (see note 2). Whether Milton and Marvell first became acquainted at this stage of their careers is not known; it is likely, I think, since Milton's letter speaks of knowing Marvell both 'by report and by the converse I have had with him', and referees tend only to invoke 'report' when there is insufficient first-hand experience to rely upon. It was, nonetheless, a strong recommendation:

there will be with you tomorrow upon some occasion of business a Gentleman whose name is Mr Marvile, a man whom both by report and the converse I have had with him of singular desert for the State to make use of, who also offers himself, if there be any employment for him. His father was the Minister of Hull, and he hath spent four years abroad in Holland, France, Italy, and Spain to very good purpose, as I believe, and the gaining of those four languages, besides he is a scholar and well-read in the Latin and Greek authors, and no doubt of an approved conversation, for he comes now lately out of the house of the Lord Fairfax, who was Generall, where he was intrusted to give some instruction in the languages to the Lady, his daughter. If upon the death of Mr Weckerlyn the Councell shall think that I shall need any assistance in the performance of my place (though for my part I find no encumbrances of that which belongs to me, except it be in point of attendence at Conferences with Ambassadors, which I must confess in my condition [Milton's blindness, now about a year old] I am not fit for) it would be hard for them to find a man so fit every way for that purpose as this gentleman... This, my Lord, I write sincerely without any other end than to perform my duty to the publick in helping them to an able servant; laying aside those jealousies and that emulation which mine own condition might suggest to me by bringing in such a coadjutor...

Milton's work consisted mainly in the civil service routines of

45 *John Milton*, crayon portrait by William Faithorne.

correspondence with foreign states, together with some propaganda for the regime. He had been assisted in this, as his letter indicates, by a German, Georg Weckherlin, who had retired owing to ill health in December 1652, whereupon his duties had been absorbed by John Thurloe, the Council's secretary. Weckherlin then died, but it was a Philip

114

Meadows not Marvell who got the post. We don't know why. Perhaps his connection with Lady Fairfax, who had inveighed against the Commission which sentenced Charles I and over which Bradshaw presided, told against him. Perhaps Marvell's authorship of 'Tom May's Death', a violently anti-Parliamentary poem, not published until 1681 (below, pp.129–32), somehow became known—though this is highly

46 *William Dutton*, portrait attributed to Lely.

improbable, there being no contemporary notice of his authorship or mention of the poem; yet equally strange rumours about his associations have come to light[56]. At any rate, Marvell had to wait for the post of Latin Secretary until 1657.

Meanwhile he found himself at Eton, tutoring William Dutton (plate 46). Cromwell had interested himself in the education of this boy, son of a Cavalier who had died in 1646 after serving in the Royalist forces, and had arranged with his uncle that William would marry Cromwell's youngest daughter, Frances, and inherit the uncle's rich estate. When this uncle died in 1657, Cromwell became William's legal guardian, but had obviously assumed responsibility for directing his education several years earlier. This involved, above all, ensuring that the boy grew up in a proper Puritan atmosphere. Hence, his sojourn at Eton and his visit, still with Marvell, to Saumur in 1656, presumably to imbibe something of the strongly Protestant intellectuality of that town.

Eton (plate 47) at this time numbered among its Fellows the Rev. John Oxenbridge, in whose home Cromwell chose to lodge William Dutton. Oxenbridge's sister had married Oliver St John as his third wife (his second had been Cromwell's cousin), and it was to St John that Marvell had addressed some ingenious Latin verses in 1651 upon his appointment as one of the Ambassadors to the United Provinces [p.99]. So perhaps St John recommended both his brother-in-law's house at Eton and Marvell as tutor for William Dutton. Marvell may also have become acquainted with Oxenbridge during the latter's lectureship at Hull in the 1640s.

John and Jane Oxenbridge had a distinguished Puritan pedigree—entirely suitable as companions for Cromwell's *de facto* ward. He had lost his Oxford tutorship under Archbishop Laud in 1634 and, together with his wife, then spent two lengthy spells in the Bermudas. Jane had been a moving spirit among the islands' Independents, and she and her husband maintained an interest in their spiritual livelihood after returning to England in 1641; in 1653 he was appointed one of the London-based commissioners for government of the colony. Their tales of the Bermudas may have prompted Marvell to compose his taut and fervent lines on the islands:

> Where the remote *Bermudas* ride
> In th'Oceans bosome unespy'd,
> From a small Boat, that row'd along,
> The listning Winds receiv'd this Song.
>   What should we do but sing his Praise
> That led us through the watry Maze,
> Unto an Isle so long unknown,
> And yet far kinder than our own?
> Where he the huge Sea-Monsters wracks,
> That lift the Deep upon their Backs.

47   Eton Chapel, engraving by Wenceslas Hollar.

> He lands us on a grassy Stage;
> Safe from the Storms, and Prelat's rage.
> He gave us this eternal Spring,
> Which here enamells every thing;
> And sends the Fowl's to us in care,
> On daily Visits through the Air.   [pp.17–18]

Ever since Shakespeare found in early writings on the Bermudas inspiration for *The Tempest*'s themes of God's providence and the wonderful metamorphosis of nature on a magic island[57], these islands have seemed a paradigm of a providential ordering both of natural disaster and of human folly into a miraculous harmony. In fact, Oxenbridge's time in the colony was fraught with much dissension and intrigue; but Marvell ignores that and charms the world of shipwreck, sea-monsters and civil war at home into the 'eternal Spring' of an Edenic world. What sustains this fine poem is his characteristic attention to contraries, here reconciled by God's care, and a new tone of religious fervour that his residence at Eton must have discovered for him:

> He cast (of which we rather boast)
> The Gospels Pearl upon our Coast.
> And in these Rocks for us did frame
> A Temple, where to sound his Name.

Oh let our Voice his Praise exalt,
Till it arrive at Heavens Vault:
Which thence (perhaps) rebounding, may
Eccho beyond the *Mexique Bay.*

'Bermudas' recalls 'The Garden' in its poetic and paradisal ecology—'He makes the Figs our mouths to meet;/And throws the Melons at our feet'. But it does not seem concerned to explore some of the other poem's paradoxes—either the impossibility of a life in Paradise or the sudden appearance of a 'skilful Gardner' in that green world. Marvell's tone in 'Bermudas', in short, seems strangely confident and single-minded in its Puritan zeal; the only gardener is God, whose art *is* nature. What is interesting to speculate is what motive or combination of motives lay behind Marvell's strongly devotional mode of utterance at this time. Was this another manifestation of the chameleon poet, adapting to the environment of Eton as much for camouflage as by conviction? Was it rather an experimental curiosity—to see what this part was like to play, but then finding the role real or congenial? Was it simply a time-serving obsequiousness, angling for public office by behaving in ways likely to attract Cromwell's attention and further patronage?

A letter Marvell addressed to Cromwell from Eton in July 1653 (from which I've taken the title of this section) seems deferential and devout:

It might perhaps seem fit for me to seek out words to give your Excellence thanks for my selfe. But indeed the onely Civility which it is proper for me to practise with so eminent a Person is to obey you, and to performe honestly the worke that you have set me about. Therefore I shall use the time that your Lordship is pleas'd to allow me for writing, onely to that purpose for which you have given me it: That is to render you some account of Mr Dutton. I have taken care to examine him severall times in the presence of Mr Oxenbridge, as those who weigh and tell over money before some witnesse ere they take charge of it. For I thought that there might possibly be some lightnesse in the Coyn, or errour in the telling, which hereafter I should be bound to make good. Therefore Mr Oxenbridge is the best to make your Excellence an impartiall relation thereof. I shall onely say that I shall strive according to my best understanding (that is according to those Rules your Lordship hath given me) to increase whatsoever Talent he may have already. Truly he is of a gentle and waxen disposition: and, God be praisd, I can not say that he hath brought with him any evill Impression, and I shall hope to set nothing upon his Spirit but what may be of a good Sculpture.   [II.304]

Yet however respectful, there is a canny precaution in his anticipating any failure with a pupil who was apparently not of the brightest, and some deft allusion to his Hull background in the mercantile imagery. But the name of God is twice invoked, and the Oxenbridge ambience duly receives its humble approbation:

But above all I shall labour to make [Dutton] sensible of his Duty to God. For then we begin to serve faithfully, when we consider that he is our Master. And in this both he and I owe infinitely to your Lordship, for having placed us in so godly a family as that of Mr Oxenbridge whose Doctrine and Example are like a Book and a Map, not onely instructing the Eare but demonstrating to the Ey which way we ought to travell. And Mrs Oxenbridge hath a great tendernesse over him also in all other things.

Such a letter is obviously not the occasion on which to reveal his scepticisms, if he had them, of this ménage. In a Latin epitaph on Jane Oxenbridge [pp.139–40] he was to notice rather urbanely what others recorded with more malice, that she proselytized among her cronies at Eton. Maybe Marvell was mentally contrasting that ministry with the larger and more spacious hymn to God of his Bermudan sailors. A more obvious indication of his less than complete identification with the Oxenbridges' devotions is his acquaintance with John Hales, who lived a few miles from Eton in an Anglican enclave at Ritchings, near Langley. He had once been Laud's chaplain, then Fellow of Eton and Canon at Windsor, but lost both posts under the Parliamentarians. When Marvell met him he was living obscurely and in poverty, and the poet later recorded his pride at having known Hales:

I reckon it not one of the least Ignominies of that Age, that so eminent a Person should have been by the Iniquity of the times reduced to those necessities under which he lived; as I account it no small honour to have grown up into some part of his Acquaintance, and convers'd a while with the living *remains* of one of the clearest heads and best prepared brests in Christendom.   [*RT*.79]

And Marvell copied into the text of his own *Rehearsal Transpros'd* a lengthy section from Hales's *Tract Concerning Schisme and Schismatiques* (1642). Whether or not Marvell already admired in the 1650s its plea for toleration and its perception that the strictness that forces schism upon others is as guilty as those who break away from the Church, he obviously must have appreciated Hales's company as an alternative to that of the Oxenbridges. Since William Dutton's aunt was also a member of the community at Ritchings, there were presumably opportunities for visits, during which his tutor could have talked with Hales. He was immensely well-read, though now without his valuable library which he had been forced to sell, 'a good poet'—at least according to Aubrey—and 'a bountiful mind' (*Brief Lives*, pp.276–7). In his last years he was forced to remove even from Ritchings and to live with a former servant, since Cromwell in 1655 forbad the harbouring of reactionaries. In this last retreat Aubrey recalls having seen him—

a prettie little man, sanguine, of a cheerful countenance, very gentile, and courteous; I was received by him with much humanity: he was in a kind of

119

violet-coloured cloath Gowne, with buttons and loopes (he wore not a black gowne) and was reading Thomas à Kempis; it was within a yeare before he deceased. He loved Canarie; but moderately, to refresh his spirits.

So Hales evidently shared unintellectual interests with Marvell, of whom Aubrey also reports (p.357) that 'He kept bottles of wine at his lodgeing, and many times he would drinke liberally by himselfe to refresh his spirits, and exalt his Muse'. Aubrey also makes it clear that 'though he loved wine he would never drinke hard in company' (p.356). At Hales's death in 1656 Marvell was abroad in France and unable to attend his funeral.

Such, then, was the range of Marvell's contacts while at Eton. He addressed Latin verses to another Eton College fellow, Nathaniel Ingelo, upon his departure as chaplain to the Ambassador to Sweden in 1653, a diplomatic manoeuvre designed to draw a neutral Sweden towards England's side in the war against Holland. Marvell must also have continued to see something of Bradshaw, who lived near Eton, for in June 1654 he is writing to Milton to explain—as an earlier letter had apparently failed to do adequately—his delivery of a copy of Milton's *Defensio Secunda* to Bradshaw. Again, we notice Marvell's studied respect and the diplomatic handling of his friend, who is evidently jealous of his reputation:

I did not satisfie my self in the Account I gave you, of presenting your Book to my Lord, although it seemed to me that I writ to you all which the Messengers speedy Returne the same night from Eaton would permit me. and I perceive that by Reason of that Hast I did not give you satisfaction neither concerning the Delivery of your Letter at the same Time. Be pleased therefore to pardon me, and know, that I tendered them both together. But my Lord read not the Letter while I was with him, which I attributed to our Despatch, and some other Businesse tending thereto, which I therefore wished ill to, so farr as it hindred an affaire much better and of greater Importance: I mean that of reading your Letter. And to tell you truly mine own Imagination, I thought that He would not open it while I was there, because He might suspect that I delivering it just upon my Departure might have brought in it some second Proposition like to that which you had before made to him by your Letter to my Advantage.

—which implies that Marvell's employment at Eton may have come as a result of Milton's recommendation—

However I assure my self that He has since read it, and you, that He did then witnesse all Respect to your person, and as much satisfaction concerning your work as could be expected from so cursory a Review and so sudden an Account as He could then have of it from me.   [pp.305–6]

Marvell also acknowledges the copies sent to Oxenbridge and to

120

48 Cromwell dismissing the Rump Parliament, engraving, 1653.

himself—'I shall now studie it even to the getting of it by Heart'.

This circle of acquaintances and friends can remind us of the complexities of alignment and allegiance among which Marvell lived, doubtless with some satisfaction to his open-mindedness. There were Independents like the Oxenbridges; disgraced Anglicans like Hales, Oliver St John, Oxenbridge's brother-in-law, had kept away from the regicide commission over which Bradshaw had presided. Bradshaw protested the dissolution of the Council of State on 20 April 1653, the day after Cromwell had dismissed the Rump Parliament (plate 48), and remained a staunch republican under the Protectorate, which was established in December that year. But Marvell is in touch with Bradshaw, friendly with Milton, another dedicated republican, and yet tutor to Cromwell's son-in-law designate (son of a Royalist) as well as warmly celebrating—as we shall see—the achievements of the Lord Protector.

In his writings at this time Marvell was also dividing his attention between poems on public affairs and those with private, spiritual concerns; between poetry in an accomplished Latinity (as if to show he was ideally fitted for the public service he still sought[58]) and that in English. Characteristically, two of the latter, possibly written in these Eton years, are cast into dialogue form. In one the 'Resolved Soul' defends its militant integrity against the challenge of 'Created Pleasure' [pp.9–12]; in the other the Soul argues, with less obvious superiority, against the Body's claims [pp.21–3]. This second debate, which may well be only a fragment of a longer dialogue that has not survived, makes the Soul's shrillness and aloofness a little ridiculous:

> O who shall, from this Dungeon, raise
> A Soul inslav'd so many wayes?
> With bolts of Bones, that fetter'd stands
> In Feet; and manacled in Hands.
> Here blinded with an Eye; and there
> Deaf with the drumming of an Ear.
> A Soul hung up, as 'twere, in Chains
> Of Nerves, and Arteries, and Veins.

The Body's retort, that medicine could never cure the maladies which the Soul forces it to undergo, also makes the Soul's regime seem less than serious:

> But Physick yet could never reach
> The Maladies Thou me dost teach;
> Whom first the Cramp of Hope does Tear:
> And then the Palsie Shakes of Fear.
> The Pestilence of Love does heat:
> Or Hatred's hidden Ulcer eat.

The Body appears to have the last word, at least in the version that has come down to us, and it invokes a familiar Marvellian argument, which the Mower had also deployed:

> What but a Soul could have the wit
> To build me up for Sin so fit?
> So Architects do square and hew,
> Green Trees that in the Forest grew.

This extreme confidence in Nature *tout simple*—like Montaigne's defence of cannibals uncorrupted by civilization—reads like another of the poet's high-spirited explorations of some logical extreme.

'A Dialogue, Between the Resolved Soul, and Created Pleasure', on the other hand, seems much more enthralled by the Puritan atmosphere of the Oxenbridges:

Your Excellencyes most humble and faithfull Servant

Courage my Soul, now learn to wield
The weight of thine immortal Shield.
Close on thy Head thy Helmet bright.
Ballance thy Sword against the Fight.
See where an Army, strong as fair,
With silken Banners spreads the air.
Now, if thou bee'st that thing Divine,
In this day's Combat let it shine...

Pleasure, courteous and deferential even when most insidious in its temptations, displays an inherent respect for the Soul, which it hails as 'Creations Guest,/Lord of Earth, and Heavens Heir'. Moreover, the very formulation of its invitations, whether sensual or intellectual, seems calculated to afford the Resolved Soul a certain and an unimpeded triumph:

Pleasure
Lay aside that Warlike Crest,
And of Nature's banquet share:
Where the Souls of fruits and flow'rs
Stand prepar'd to heighten yours.

Soul
I sup above, and cannot stay
To bait so long upon the way.

...

Pleasure
Thou shalt know each hidden Cause;
And see the future Time:
Try what depth the Centre draws;
And then to Heaven climb.

Soul
None thither mounts by the degree
Of Knowledge, but Humility.

We have seen Marvell's studied humility towards Cromwell in his new post as godly tutor to young William Dutton. Doubtless the traditional military imagery of the soul's warfare ('for still new Charges sound'), that derives from Paul's exhortations to the Ephesians vi.16–7, recovered fresh point in the context of a Civil War that was fought and won by a general so firmly convinced of God's working through him. The two Latin epigrams upon portraits of the Lord Protector [p.108] also invoke these military dimensions of the new regime, the first reminding the viewers of the portrait that Cromwell's image puts enemies to flight but

123

allows citizens to enjoy a peaceful leisure, the second, sent to the Queen of Sweden, making the same point more ponderously:

> Sicque *Senex* Armis impiger Ora fero;
> Invia Fatorum dum per Vestigia nitor,
> Exequor et Populi fortia Jussa Manu.

(Thus an old man, yet vigorous, I face my enemies, while I press through the pathless tracks of the Fates and execute the strong commands of the people with force.)

Marvell's writings at this time explore both the triumphs of a spiritual crown—'The Coronet' [pp.14–15] and 'On a Drop of Dew' [pp.12–13] may also date from this period of emphatic Puritanism—and the responsibilities and glories of earthly rule. On the one hand; he attends to his soul's education; on the other, to his political ambitions. In 'On a Drop of Dew' the soul recalls

> still its former height,
> Shuns the sweat leaves and blossoms green;
> And, recollecting its own Light,
> Does, in its pure and circling thoughts, express
> The greater Heaven in an Heaven less.

(The Latin version of this theme, 'Ros' [pp.13–14], is much less emphatically Christian.) Yet other poems focus just as fervently upon the lesser Heaven of political life. During the years 1651–4 Marvell wrote four times (twice in Latin) on public affairs, showing himself properly appreciative of Cromwell's foreign policy.

We have seen that he addressed Oliver St John on his appointment to the embassy sent to negotiate an alliance with the Dutch. The lines [p.99] play with the addressee's names, asking the Dutch whether they want peace (the olive branch, Oliver) or war (the apostle John, son of thunder): 'Vultis Oliverum, Batavi, Sanctumve Johannem?' The ambassadors returned in June 1651, having failed in their negotiations, and six months later Parliament passed the Navigation Act, which provided that all foreign goods should be imported into England in English ships. This struck deliberately at the Dutch supremacy in commercial carrying, in particular at the Dutch shipping used by those colonies, Virginia and the Barbadoes, which had remained loyal to the Royalist cause. War was declared in 1652. By the following year, when Marvell probably wrote 'The Character of Holland', the English fleets had successfully dominated the Channel and virtually paralysed the huge port of Amsterdam. As a Hull man Marvell presumably had shipping interests very much at heart, and his poem culminates in a scathing, sometimes

49   Medal commemorating the Dutch War, 1654.

facetious, attack on Dutch naval power—'Their Navy all our Conquest or our Wreck':

> For while our *Neptune* doth a *Trident* shake,
> Steel'd with those piercing Heads, *Dean, Monck and Blake*.
> And while Jove governs in the highest Sphere,
> Vainly in *Hell* let *Pluto* domineer.

The low-lying landscape of Holland (what Howell's *Instructions... for Forren Travell* had termed 'a People planted as it were under the *Sea*', p.89) gives Marvell the chance to equate the country with the underworld.

The Dutch War did not end until 1654, but its success, including the Dutch submission to the Navigation Act, always impressed Marvell, who would subsequently come to compare Charles II's humiliations in the second Dutch War with the energies of the Protector, 'Whose navies hold the sluices of the sea'[59] (plate 49).

A diplomatic mission was sent in September 1653 to try and win over Sweden's neutrality and gain her friendship during the Dutch War (this was successfully managed, and a treaty was signed in Uppsala in April the following year). One of Marvell's new Eton friends, Ingelo, accompanied the Ambassador Extraordinary, Bulstrode Whitlocke, as chaplain, and the poet addressed him in Latin verses which turn a personal address into public flattery of Queen Christina and some elegant propaganda for the English cause. Doubtless Marvell hoped the Queen would see the verses, aiming, as Legouis put it[60], to prove that a Puritan could possess all the graces of a Cavalier. Not only does the poet flatter the Swedish state—'Pace vigil, Bello strenua, justa Foro' (Vigilant in peace, vigorous in war, just in trade)—but he emphasizes the piety and learning of its Queen which have made the country a home for the muses and temples for God ('Musarumque domus, et sua Templa Deo'). Her humanistic skills, in particular, which the Latin verses acknowledge in kind, are said to make every grove resound with Roman song ('Carmine Romuleo sic strepit omne Nemus'). And this leads in its turn to a fantasy—Cavalier enough—upon her portrait, which has been sent to Cromwell, in whose chiaroscuro ('mistasque Coloribus Umbras') the poet imagines a whole world of mythological, almost libertine, conceits. If it was indeed Marvell's poem that was shown to the Queen, according to Whitlocke's *Journale* it pleased her hugely. Its vision of her sympathetic attention to England's embassy was realized in the Uppsala treaty, and it may be that the poem's exuberant and skilful panegyric played a part in convincing the Queen:

> Dicitur et nostros moerens audisse Labores,
> Fortis et ingenuam Gentis amasse Fidem.
> Oblatae Batavam nec paci commodat Aurem;
> Nec versat Danos insidiosa dolos.

(She is said, lamenting, to have heard of our travails and to have loved the free-born faith of a brave people. Nor does she please the Dutch ear with an offer of Peace, or, deceitful, consider Danish tricks.)

After the poem to Ingelo, Marvell's next work, 'The First Anniversary of the Government under O.C.' [pp.108–19], is less, or less immediately, engaging. Unlike the others, which were probably kept under revision during his lifetime, this was printed by Thomas Newcomb, the Government printer, and published *instanter* in 1655[61]. Its purpose was obviously to laud the Protector's vigorous achievements—

> 'Tis he the force of scatter'd Time contracts,
> And in one Year the work of Ages acts

—to justify the Protectorate at home and abroad, at the same time expending some satiric vigour of its own on the government's enemies, and even (though covertly) to hint at the idea of Cromwell's assuming the crown. To review Cromwell's first year as Protector posed problems of poetic coherence, as Marvell himself notes—

> Let this one Sorrow interweave among
> The other Glories of our yearly Song

—and problems of political integrity in commentator (the poet) and 'the ruling Instrument' (the government). The overall structure of the poem relies, as Wallace (p.137) has shown, upon traditional rhetorical divisions, whereby a theme is introduced, divided into sections, defended against rival arguments, enlivened by digressions, even diatribes, and finally shaped into a peroration. Such shapes are perhaps difficult to recognize these days. But they are reinforced and sustained, even italicized, as it were, for modern ears, by patterns of imagery and modulations of tone, which go some way to unifying the verses.

Cromwell's whole career is seen in the context of time and the times. The 'Ode' four years earlier had both taken note of Cromwell's 'industrious Valour', which Marvell still recognizes as his guiding genius, and seen it 'ruine the great Work of Time,/And cast the Kingdome old/Into another Mold'. Now the Protector has to work energetically to contract, outpace, even anticipate time:

> And still the Day which he doth next restore,
> Is the just Wonder of the Day before.

Marvell alludes several times during the poem to Cromwell's dismissal of the Rump Parliament because of its ineffective slowness:

> tedious Statesmen many years did hack,
> Framing a Liberty that still went back.

By contrast, Cromwell's energy leads his countrymen forward to a new stability and a new harmony. This harmony ('all compos'd by his attractive Song') observes the large time of celestial and musical diapason and the local time of contemporary exigency. (The architectural images allow both these and other senses, reconciling engineering stresses into a whole building, or the harmonious proportions of Renaissance architectural theory and practice[62] to the practical demands of client and materials.) This local pressure from the times involves Cromwell, and his poet, in further reconciling the expectations and traditions of history—biblical allusions predominate in this poem—to the demands of a new and unestablished state. The implication, as Shakespeare put it[63], is that those who innovate or rebel against established order must 'work on leases of short-numbered hours'. Cromwell and England barely have sufficient time to consolidate their new Commonwealth:

> Hence oft I think, if in some happy Hour
> High Grace should meet in one with highest Pow'r,
> And then a seasonable People still
> Should bend to his, as he to Heavens will,
> What we might hope, what wonderfull Effect
> From such a wish'd Conjuncture might reflect.
> Sure, the mysterious Work, where none withstand,

> Would forthwith finish under such a Hand:
> Fore-shortned Time its useless Course would stay,
> And soon precipitate the latest Day.

The poet's panegyrical tone readily modulates into a millennial vision. Indeed, it is the poet's special art to penetrate the clouds that still conceal Cromwell's significance from mortal sight and prevent men from determining that 'If these the Times, then this must be the Man'. But ordinary men abroad (this elicits the poet's scorn) and at home (this, his sorrow) do not care and 'Look on, all unconcern'd, or unprepar'd'. Since the poet's function is to survey present times and larger historical perspectives, this general unconcern is highlighted by recalling the accident that had befallen Cromwell in September 1654, when the coach and team of six great horses he was driving in Hyde Park were upset. The incident made for much anxiety about the political vacuum ('Nature that hateth emptiness', as the 'Ode' put it) that Cromwell's sudden death would create, destroying all his contributions to the new stability. Nobody could adequately fill his place. While that thought is uppermost in Marvell's mind, the possibility that an hereditary succession would ensure the continuation of the new state is mooted but not, at this point, emphasized:

> Thou with the same strength, and an Heart as plain,
> Didst (like thine Olive) still refuse to Reign.

The difficulty perhaps is that those not privileged like the poet cannot adjudicate the present state of government:

> 'Tis not a Freedome, that where All command;
> Nor Tyranny, where One does them withstand:
> But who of both the Bounders knows to lay
> Him as their Father must the State obey.

The poem has to this point maintained a various, but generally moderate tone—some awe at Cromwell's skilful role as the 'headstrong Peoples Charioteer', some knowing millennial confidence and, accordingly, some slightly melodramatic dismay at his near escape from death. But the difficulties involved in appreciating the Lord Protector's special position, the subtleties of which evidently enthral Marvell, provoke a vicious attack on those many sectarians (Fifth Monarchists, Ranters, Familists, even Quakers) who threaten Cromwell's success:

> The Shame and Plague both of the Land and Age,
> Who watch'd thy halting, and thy Fall deride,
> Rejoycing when thy Foot had slipt aside;

Your Excellencyes most humble and faithfull Servant

> That their new King might the fifth Scepter shake,
> And make the World, by his Example, Quake
>
> . . .
>
> Accursed Locusts, whom your King does spit
> Out of the Center of th'unbottom'd Pit;
> Wand'rers, Adult'rers, Lyers, *Munser's* rest,
> Sorcerers, Atheists, Jesuites, Possest;
> You who the Scriptures and the Laws deface
> With the same liberty as Points and Lace.

Their hostility and incomprehension are as ignorant as early man's superstitions about the sun (thus returning the poem to its first image of the 'Sun-like' Cromwell, and enacting the daily restoration of its light). But with a dramatic extension of such uninformed perspectives Marvell imagines the incredulities of foreign Princes:

> 'He seems a King by long Succession born,
> 'And yet the same to be a King does scorn.
> 'Abroad a King he seems, and something more,
> 'At Home a Subject on the equal Floor.'

The difficulty of judging and explaining Cromwell's achievement becomes, in fact, a measure of his success. The poet has a special insight—demonstrated by his confident attack upon the 'Accursed Locusts' of the opposition at home and by his understanding résumé of puzzled foreign reactions. And he turns this superior vision to advantage in Cromwell's cause:

> Pardon, great Prince, if thus their Fear or Spight
> More then our Love and Duty do thee Right.

The poem ends by recalling the imagery with which it started, the troubled waters of time closing peacefully over human events, and explains them in an image that makes Cromwell a healer and thus a victor over time even as he is still its servant:

> And as the *Angel* of our Commonweal,
> Troubling the Waters, yearly mak'st them Heal.

One of the unaccountable problems of Marvell's literary and political career in the early 1650s is how these unconstrained praises of Cromwell and other Commonwealth figures can issue so quickly upon the heels of 'Tom May's Death' [pp.94–7], just as that poem itself perplexingly followed fast after the 'Horatian Ode'. May had been a Royalist who switched his allegiance to Parliament during the Civil War, became the historian of the Long Parliament and even published the seized correspondence of Charles (*The King's Cabinet Opened* of 1645). Not surprisingly he was loathed by Royalists, so that Marvell's satire upon his death, together with the poem's attack upon all Parliamentarians under the Roman metaphors of Brutus, Cassius and Spartacus, allies the poet with the Royalists. Yet, since May died on 13 November 1650, it means that 'Tom May's Death' must have been composed soon after the 'Ode', with its approval, however qualified, of Cromwell, and even composed, too, under Fairfax's roof. What is also surprising about the poem, as Christine Rees has pointed out[64], is that it seems to abandon the subtle poetics and politics of the 'Ode' in favour of the 'commoner front-line tactics of the paper war'.

The puzzle cannot really be solved. The very fact of 'Tom May's Death' lends strong support to those who read the 'Ode' as implying strong reservations about Cromwell's rise to power. It also reinforces our sense of Marvell's characteristic exploration of alternative ideas and states; for even if this piece was composed just before joining the Fairfaxes in Yorkshire, it is still a resonant example of his retaining a strictly private dimension to his career, for it was not apparently published until 1681, nor could it ever have been shown at either Nun Appleton or later at Eton. After the Restoration it may have been circulated, and there is some distinct indication that Marvell was revising it then, for lines 85–7 seem to allude to the fact that, though buried in Westminster Abbey, for which a grateful Council of State voted £100, May's remains were disinterred in September 1661. There are other hints that the poem was revised in the light of new conditions after 1660—the tolerance extended to other republicans in lines 55–6. Yet the poem's basic fiction—May's drunken arrival among the Elysian shades—argues for composition soon after his death. So that in the absence of any further evidence we must take the poem as an expression of Marvell's continuing and private assessment of the public world of politics, in this case especially its inconsistencies. In the 'First Anniversary' he would commiserate with Cromwell—

> For all delight of Life thou then didst lose,
> When to Command, thou didst they self Depose;
> Resigning up thy Privacy so dear,
> To turn the headstrong Peoples Charioteer.

Marvell himself was able to retain such a privacy for himself, and 'Tom May's Death' takes advantage of that privilege.

The poem certainly begins by expressing contempt for May's excesses in one of the delights of life. Marvell, who Aubrey said would 'never drinke hard in company', mocks a man who died, again according to Aubrey, 'after drinking with his chin tyed with his cap (being fatt); suffocated'. But the shade whom he takes for a publican turns out to be

Ben Jonson's ghost, and thereupon the poem enlarges its theme. By making Jonson repudiate May—an apt device, for May had hoped to succeed Jonson as Poet Laureate in 1637—Marvell makes the poem as much a matter of poetic as of political integrity. The two are related, of course, in a man's life, and the use as May's accuser here of Jonson, an examplar of the necessary connection between good art and good life, is particularly telling. He criticizes May's pretensions to being either a poet or a political commentator (for 'Ben' is 'Sworn Enemy to all that do pretend'). As a poet May is banished from the company of such as Homer, Virgil, Chaucer and Spenser; as a political theorist he is rejected along with other 'novice Statesmen'. He compounds these disabilities when he invokes inadequate Roman analogies for current English events:

> Far from these blessed shades tread back agen
> Most servil' wit, and Mercenary Pen.
> *Polydore, Lucan, Allan, Vandale, Goth,*
> Malignant Poet and Historian both.
> Go seek the novice Statesmen, and obtrude
> On them some Romane cast similitude.

Marvell, of course, had himself found striking Roman colour for his 'Horatian Ode' just before May's death, even perhaps borrowing from May's translation of Lucan to do so. Whether Marvell here wishes merely to say that such analogies must, like his own, make real sense or to voice a bold antithesis to or even revulsion from his own practice, May's gravest fault seems to be his failure to see proper connections between republican Rome and Commonwealth England and accordingly his failure to maintain his integrity as a poet in a world where all activity is finally political:

> When the Sword glitters ore the Judges head,
> And fear has Coward Churchmen silenced,
> Then is the Poets time, 'tis then he drawes,
> And single fights forsaken Vertues cause.
> He, when the wheel of Empire, whirleth back,
> And though the World's disjointed Axel crack,
> Sings still of ancient Rights and better Times,
> Seeks wretched good, arraigns successful Crimes.

This stirring call to the poet to see steadily and whole and to speak out is a dramatic speech by the Jonson of the poem; it also seems to bear Marvell's *imprimatur*. But it is worth remarking that on the evidence of the 'Ode' Marvell had not yet practised what he lets Jonson preach. Maybe these lines, too, are a Restoration addition or represent a revision in the light of his Cromwell panegyrics of the 1650s. It is certain that within a few years of May's drunken death Marvell followed Ben Jonson's precept and 'varied streight his Song,/Gently to signifie that he was wrong'. Legouis thinks he was finally converted to Cromwell's side by the success of the Dutch War. The opening of the 'First Anniversary', as has been observed[65], neatly disposes of Charles I's death *and* Marvell's previous commitments in its invocation of the waters of oblivion:

> Like the vain Curlings of the Watry maze,
> Which in smooth streams a sinking Weight does raise;
> So Man, declining alwayes, disappears
> In the weak Circles of increasing Years;
> And his short Tumults of themselves Compose,
> While flowing Time above his Head does close.

From the advertisement for 'The First Anniversary' in *Mercurius Politicus* of 11–18 January 1655 until the next year we know nothing of Marvell's life. In January 1656 he reappears, with William Dutton, at Saumur on the Loire[66]. The town was famous for its Protestant Académie and Collège (a kind of university and grammar school respectively), though it seems doubtful whether Dutton would have been enrolled in either of them. His tutor, on the other hand, must have participated eagerly in the intellectual life of this community, if we may judge on the basis of some fragmentary references. He obviously reported to Milton, by now well aware of his friend's love of fame, that his *Pro se Defensio* was much in demand, for Milton sent copies the following year to another Englishman for distribution. Yet there had been much antagonism from French Protestants to the execution of Charles I, so that Marvell must have had to engage in some vigorous defence of Cromwell, whose intended son-in-law Dutton was already known to be. That he got involved in disputations when Milton's propaganda writings came up indicates that he did not shirk those opportunities in either Protestant or Catholic circles. Indeed, he was to record later his appreciation of some Roman Catholics in terms that perhaps recall his stay at Saumur:

For although we live under a rationall jealousie alwaies of Popery, yet whatsoever is said by any author of that persuasion, is not forthwith therefore to be clamorously rejected. Have not there constantly been among them, men fit to be owned for holy life, good sense, good learning?   [Grosart, IV.236]

Saumur was indeed widely noted for its religious toleration, and Marvell's own tastes in such matters were obviously strengthened by his stay there.

Marvell and Dutton were still at Saumur in August 1656, but nothing is heard of the former again until early the following summer, when he composed the lines 'On the Victory obtained by Blake over the Spaniards' [pp.119–24]. The poem appears with Marvell's other works in

Miscellaneous Poems in 1681 (having also been printed twice before, in 1674 and 1678), but is hardly their equal. Blake, who brought off a remarkable engagement by capturing sixteen treasure ships at Tenerife, is barely allowed into the poem; instead, Marvell addresses himself—without actually mentioning any name—to Cromwell, 'That boundless Empire, where you give the Law'. Blake's boldness actually won the treasure, but Marvell insists that 'your resistless genious there did Raign'. It is all rather blatant flattery, at least from Marvell, and it is perhaps significant that he now commits himself without qualification to the plea that Cromwell should assume the crown—'The best of Lands should have the best of Kings'. There are flashes of some better Marvellian wit, notably the conceit of the stupendous hill at Tenerife inhabiting 'Earth and Heaven', but the verses are otherwise flaccid and padded out. Perhaps it was a studied manoeuvre to gain the Latin Secretaryship. It is an even worse thought that it succeeded precisely in that aim, for by September 1657 Marvell's appointment to that post took effect.

His duties in Thurloe's office earned him a salary of £200 a year. They consisted mostly of correspondence—assuring petitioners, for example, that the matter of collecting funds for Protestant refugees from Bohemia was in hand or writing, on Thurloe's instructions, to the King of Portugal about the ill-treatment of the Scottish 'Guinea Company' at San Tome[67] His talents as a linguist were also relied upon in receiving foreign envoys. It was, in all, a post that gave him some first-hand administrative experience in an efficient Government office, although he was later to represent it in a slightly different light, describing 'an imployment, for which I was not altogether improper, and which I consider'd to be the most innocent and inoffensive toward his Majesties affairs of any in that usurped and irregular Government, to which all men were then exposed' [*RT*.203]. The new post brought him, too, into closer personal contact with Cromwell, as his next two poetic compositions reveal.

The first was two songs performed at the marriage of the Protector's third daughter, Mary, to Thomas Belasyse, second Viscount Fauconberg, a Yorkshireman and kinsman of Fairfax. The pastoral songs [pp.125–9] first represent the bridegroom as Endymion wooing the reluctant Cynthia (Marvell reverses their mythological roles of wooer and wooed) and being urged by the Chorus to take encouragement from her 'younger sister', Frances Cromwell, who had married the heir of the Earl of Warwick a week earlier. (This was the daughter originally destined for William Dutton, whose fortunes seem readily forgotten by his former tutor.) To the pleasant invention of making Endymion the suitor—a proper tribute perhaps to the dignity of the Lord Protector's daughter—Marvell adds a witty enough exchange, reminiscent of his earlier debates:

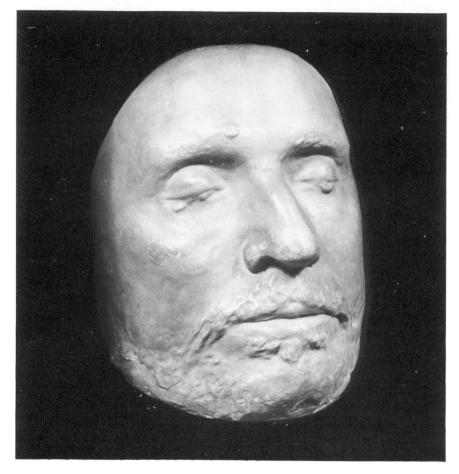

50   Death mask of Oliver Cromwell.

Endymion
Here unto *Latmos Top* I climbe:
How far below thine *Orbe* sublime?
O why, as well as Eyes to see,
Have I not Armes that reach to thee?

Cynthia
'Tis needless then that I refuse,
Would you but your own Reason use.

Endymion
Though I so high may not pretend,
It is the same so you descend.

134

The second song, in which shepherds prepare to greet the couple and lament that a November wedding prevents their gathering garlands (the bride being 'the only flow'r'), seems even gently to mock its own pastoral mode and the masque-like occasion:

> *Phillis*
> *He* so looks as fit to keep
> Somewhat else then silly *Sheep.*

Perhaps such a note allows a Commonwealth event to resume something of a Royalist celebration without taking itself too seriously.

Marvell's next poem has a sadder theme, for on 3 September 1658 Oliver Cromwell died (plate 50). It was the anniversary of his battles at Dunbar in 1650 and at Worcester in 1651. Yet the predominant tone of the poem is not of public lament, but of a fine personal sorrow: 'Nor though a *Prince* to be a *Man* refus'd'. The poet necessarily attends to Cromwell's public career, but even here the emphasis is upon its inward virtues and integrity: 'Valour, religion, friendship, prudence dy'd/At once with him, and all that's good beside'. 'A Poem upon the Death of O.C.' [pp.129–37] is coloured throughout by a very personal sadness, which permeates even the apostrophes to Cromwell's military life and culminates in Marvell's explicitly personal testimony:

> I saw him dead, a leaden slumber lyes,
> And mortal sleep over those wakefull eyes:
> Those gentle rays under the lids were fled,
> Which through his looks that piercing sweetnesse shed;
> That port which so majestique was and strong,
> Loose and depriv'd of vigour, stretch'd along:
> All wither'd, all discolour'd, pale and wan,
> How much another thing, no more that man?

Earlier in the poem it was Cromwell's family affections, especially towards his second daughter, Elizabeth, who had died in August 1658, that gave the poem its special tone. The family scenes, the intuitions of each other's affections and distress ('She lest He grieve hides what She can her pains,/And He to lessen hers his Sorrow feigns'), sound a quite rare note in Marvell; not only do they confess an intimacy with the Protector's family and a strongly personal devotion to Cromwell by the time of his death, but they also reveal how the poet could occasionally set aside his predilection for intricacy of response and testify to an uncomplicated admiration.

The poem was entered in the *Stationers' Register* as due to appear in a volume with similar offerings by Dryden and Sprat. But the project did not materialize, and another printer issued it with a poem by Edmund

Waller instead of Marvell's (see I.332n). Thus Marvell's lament remained aptly private until 1681 and even then did not really see the light of day (see below, p.190). Waller's and Dryden's items are much more routine and predictable than Marvell's[68]. The first speaks briefly, connecting Cromwell's death with a recent storm before offering a rather restrained survey of his achievements. The second is more fulsome, more determinately public in its canvas of England's historical fortunes under Cromwell's rule. Its feeling is often contrived, like some of its imagery:

> No Civill broyles have since his death arose,
> But *Faction* now by *Habit* does obey:
> And *Warrs* have that respect for his repose,
> As *Winds* for *Halcyons* when they breed at Sea.

It was true that no upheavals followed the Protector's death, as Marvell had feared when he wrote the 'First Anniversary'. He can record now that Cromwell's son, Richard, continues where his father left off; with a glance perhaps at the 'Horatian Ode' (still unpublished) Marvell notes that 'He, as his father, long was kept from sight/In private...' There is some attempt to retain the domestic emphases from earlier in the poem. It is probably only hindsight that suggests to us today that Marvell works a little too hard at making Richard's succession auspicious.

The Privy Council voted Marvell, as it did Milton, six yards of black cloth for his mourning. Dryden did not obtain this, though he was actually their colleague in Thurloe's office. For none of them would the next two years be easy or free from anxiety—Milton would find himself briefly in prison when the monarchy was restored; Dryden had to live down his fulsome praise of Cromwell. Marvell survived best of them all, with a buoyancy that should not surprise us, even if we cannot altogether account for it.

8 A Landskip of our Mottly Parliament

Marvell continued as Latin Secretary at least until February 1660, maybe even longer. From January 1659 he was also Member of Parliament for Hull, and he continued to represent his birthplace in the Commons until

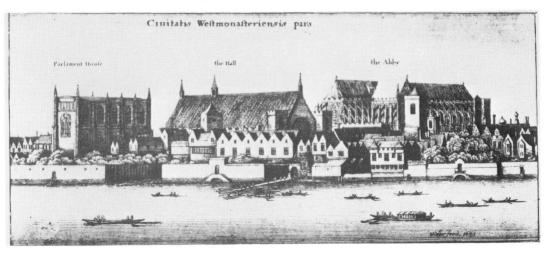

Ciuitatis Weſtmonaſterienſis pars

Parliament Houſe   the Hall   the Abby

51   View of Westminster, engraving by Wenceslas Hollar.

his death in 1678. His life for these final twenty years was, then, centred upon Westminster Hall (plate 51), where the Parliament met[69]. He had two spells away: one for a few months in Holland; another, more exotically, on a diplomatic mission to Moscow. He seems to have served his constituents well, reporting faithfully to them on parliamentary business (nearly three hundred letters to the Hull Corporation survive). He also corresponded with the officers of the Trinity House at Hull (plate 52), the chief authority of the port there, mostly upon shipping matters; he was engaged, too, with the London Trinity House, of which he was elected a Younger Warden in 1678. Among these public affairs we catch glimpses of a private life, visiting friends, like Milton or the fourth Lord Wharton, escaping to his cottage in Highgate (plate 53) 'to injoy the spring and my privacy' [II.328], or simply corresponding with his nephew, William Popple, who had settled in Bordeaux about 1670. Perhaps as some mediation between his formal parliamentary career and his personal commitments, he also engaged vigorously in the paper wars that raged outside Parliament, contributing anonymous verse satires, largely on foreign affairs, in the 1660s and extensive prose pamphlets in the 1670s, when the issue of religious toleration became so acute. These writings, nowhere near so subtle and incisive as the lyric poetry for which he is best known, are the utterances of a deeply principled man who may have found the intrigues and subterfuges of the political world ultimately frustrating and compromising. The violence that had showed itself in some of the early verse or upon Flecknoe's staircase in Rome bursts out again in brawls in the Commons and was perhaps released in the tough,

52   Fragment of letter from Marvell to Trinity House, Hull, 1670.

often raw, aggression of his satires. The life of a man who immersed himself so in Restoration politics and controversy was rarely safe: Marvell's opponents often expressed surprise that he had not been physically attacked; his death, after publishing *An Account of the Growth of Popery*, was ascribed to poisoning by the Jesuits.

Marvell began by adhering firmly to Richard Cromwell's protectorate and opposing the republican opposition, represented by Sir Henry Vane, Hull's M.P. in the Long Parliament. He wrote on Thurloe's instructions in February 1659 to the English agent at The Hague, George Downing, to explain the opposition's tactics and philosophy:

Their Doctrine hath moved most upon their Maxime that all pow'r is in the people That it is reverted into this house by the death of his Highnesse [i.e. Oliver Cromwell], that Mr Speaker is Protector in possession and it will not be his wisdome to part with it easily, that this house is all England. Yet they pretend that they are for a single person and this single person but without negative voice without militia not upon the petition and advice but by adoption and donation of this House and that all the rights of the people should be specifyd and indorsed upon that Donation. But we know well enough what they mean. A Petition from some thousands in the City to their purpose hath been brought in (& they say they are trying to promote another in the Army)...   [II.307]

But the young Protector succumbed to pressures from the Army and

53 Marvell's Highgate cottage before demolition in 1868.

dissolved the Parliament on 22 April. In May the Rump resumed its sittings, with Vane as the Member for Hull, and Marvell presumably retreated to his secretaryship. He was elected junior member for Hull again in April 1660, together with John Ramsden, and he returned to a now ardently Royalist House. When the Restoration of Charles II was determined, he seems to have survived without his previous political career in Thurloe's office endangering him, as it did Milton. He seems, too, to have accepted the King's return as the best solution to the vacuum occasioned by Cromwell's death and the quarrels between Army and Parliament that succeeded it. With the active intervention of General Monck and others like Marvell's former employer, Fairfax, the King was invited back to England. He departed from Holland in style (plate 54) and arrived in London on 29 May, when Ramsden and Marvell are found writing to the Commissioners of Militia in Hull 'though it be the day of the Kings arrivall' [p.309].

In the Commons Marvell was soon variously engaged in supporting the King and pleading for Milton, though this action arose presumably from friendship rather than a continuing commitment to Commonwealth politics. He argued for Milton's release from prison without having to pay the excessive fees demanded of him. He was still defending Milton in 1673 and with as careful a manoeuvre as he must have needed to employ in 1660:

CAROLI II REGIS MAGNÆ BRITANNIÆ EX

54   Charles II leaving Holland for England in 1660, engraving by P.H. Schut.

J.M. was, and is, a man of great Learning and Sharpness of wit as any man. It was his misfortune, living in a tumultuous time, to be toss'd on the wrong side, and he writ *Flagrante bello* certain dangerous Treatises... At His Majesties happy Return, *J.M.* did partake, even as you your self did for all your huffing, of his Regal Clemency and has ever since expiated himself in a retired silence.   [*RT*.312]

The same month that he raised Milton's case in the House he acted as teller for the 'ayes' in the division on a bill enacting the King's promise of indulgence to Protestant Nonconformists. The bill was defeated, but Marvell is here seen supporting both the King and his own sense of necessary toleration: he reported to Hull that 'there is an end of that bill and for those excellent things therein We must henceforth rely onely upon his Majestyes goodnesse who I must needs say hath hitherto been more ready to give then we to receive' [p.6].

These reports sent up to Hull touch upon metropolitan gossip, on the one hand ('the Princess Henrietta... the meazles being thick upon her': p.17), and offer detailed accounts of parliamentary business, on the other, with special emphasis upon those matters that evidently concerned his constituents—taxes, excise, commerce, the militia, and religious legislation:

A Committee was orderd to inquire into the growth of Popery & to bring an Act in to prevent it. The Jews were also added into the Question. Yesterday we had a free Conference of severall hours with the Lords about...   [p.130]

Since my last, the Bill for wearing of Woollen hath been read the third time, past, and sent up to the Lords. Also the Bill for continuing the new Impost upon Wines & Vinegars hath been read the first time.   [p.243]

He writes at length, saying that 'It is hard for me to write short to you' [p.17]. He uses also a dry, even tone that allows no tremor of emotion—which surely he must have felt—as he passes from routine into serious matters:

In the Afternoon the Committee perfected the bill of Sales to be offerd to the house but I doubt much there will not be time nor inclination enough to pass it this Parl^t To day our house was upon the Bill of Attaindor of those had have bin executed, those that are fled, & of Cromwell Bradshaw Ireton & Pride And tis orderd that the Carkasses & coffins of the foure last named shall be drawn, with w^t expedition possible, upon an hurdle to Tyburn, ther be hangd up for a while & then buryed under the gallows. The Act for the Militia hath not been calld for of late men not being forward to confirme such perpetuall & exorbitant powrs by a law as it would be in danger if that Bill should be carryed on. Tis better to trust his M^{tyes} moderation...   [p.7]

The sang-froid with which the central piece of news is communicated there is explained perhaps by a determination to weather the change of administration safely and not find his past catching up with him, or it may be that his early confidence in Charles II (the letter dates from December 1660, before the Convention Parliament was dissolved) required him to tolerate such indignities to his former colleagues. But it is also part of his studied epistolary style in communicating with the Mayor and Corporation. Just occasionally, he allows himself a flash of humour—'an Act in which of all others your corporation is the least concerned: that is where wives shall refuse to cohabit with their husbands, that in such case the husband shall not be liable to pay any debts...' [p.1]. Otherwise he keeps his own opinions to himself, not even giving many hints of how he voted in the House. Yet he is eager to underline his own diligence on Hull's behalf and to point out his 'same vigour and alacrity in your businesse' [p.34]. He doesn't hesitate to tell them that he is writing on an empty stomach [p.195]. Yet, unless his tongue is wickedly in his cheek, he obviously derived satisfaction from this ceaseless correspondence: 'Tis much refreshment to me after our long sittings daily to give you account what we do' [p.6]. Perhaps this evening composition of dispatches, like his satires, though in different vein, provided a release of the tensions and annoyances of political life. The length of the letters, which he says he cannot control, like the loose and baggy satires, is perhaps a means of unburdening himself of pent-up anxieties and animosities.

These even increased in the new, Cavalier Parliament, to which Marvell was returned for Hull, this time without Ramsden, who was defeated; his colleague was a Royalist, Colonel Anthony Gilby, who had suffered imprisonment and, in the period leading up to the Restoration, acted as secret agent for the King's side. Marvell probably felt increasingly isolated in this Royalist Parliament: we know that he quarrelled with his fellow M.P., 'the bonds of civility betwixt Colonell Gilby and my selfe being unhappily snappd in pieces, and in such manner that I can not see how it is possible ever to knit them again' [p.27]; he aroused the animosity of the new Governor of Hull, a former Cavalier soldier and a Roman Catholic[70]; he had an altercation with a fellow member, the Royalist Clifford, and refusing at first to admit that he gave the initial provocation was censored by an evidently partial Speaker. Marvell was to remember them both in his poems a few years later.

Doubtless his quarrel with Gilby made him more than usually sensitive to his reputation back in Hull, where he urges them 'to listen to no litle storyes concerning my selfe' [p.32]. He had been from the first eager to forestall criticism of his conduct of their affairs: the first letter that survives to the Mayor and Aldermen reassures them that 'At my late absence out of Town I had taken such order that if you had commanded me any thing I might soon have received it & so returned on purpose to this place to have obeyed you' [p.1]. Now in 1662 he was having to explain another absence, this time to the Masters of Trinity House, Hull:

> But that wch troubles me is that by the interest of some persons too potent for me to refuse & who have a great direction & influence upon my counsells & fortune I am obliged to go beyond sea before I have perfected it. But first I do thereby make my Lord of Carlile (who is a member of the Privy Council & one of them to whom your businesse is referd) absolutely yours. And my journy is but into Holland from whence I shall weekly correspond even as if I were at London with all the rest of my friends toward the effecting your businesse. Then I leave Colonell Gilby here whose ability for businesse and affection to yours is such that I can not be wanted though I am missing.   [p.250]

It is assumed that this pressing business was political, even undercover. The Privy Counsellor mentioned had been a dedicated servant of the Protector, which explains Marvell's contact with him. But Marvell also had 'private concernments of mine' [p.34] to delay him in Holland: these may have been some involvement with the Presbyterian exiles gathered in Holland[71]. He would also have enjoyed renewing his knowledge of a country he had not seen for twenty years; he stayed with Downing at The Hague, but presumably travelled as well, since one of his letters is sent from Vianen, where in the 1640s he might have seen the Count of Brederode's gardens (see above, p.37). His absence in Holland, however, was eventually to displease his constituents, for in March 1663 he was writing to assure them of his 'making all the speed possible back, and that with Gods assistance in a very short time you may expect to heare of me at the Parliament House' [p.34].

Yet their apparent reprimand obviously did not weigh too long or too heavily with Marvell, for within four months he is wanting to be off again, since, as he told the Mayor, 'there is a probability I may very shortly have occasion again to go beyond sea. For my Lord Carlisle being chosen by his Majesty his Embassadour Extraordinary to Muscovy Sweden and Denmarke hath used his power which ought to be very great with me to make me goe along with him Secretary in those Embassages' [p.37–8]. Since the mission to Russia was essentially to seek the restoration of certain trading privileges which English merchants had formerly enjoyed in Russia, the aldermen and merchants of Hull were doubtless pleased to see their M.P. included in the enterprise.

He obtained 'speciall leave' of the House for his absence [p.38] and wrote farewell letters to the Hull Corporation and the Trinity House on 20 July [pp.39 and 254]. He sailed two days later, not returning until 30 January 1665—longer than the year he had estimated. The expedition was huge, filling two ships with nearly eighty persons (including two trumpeters, a surgeon, six musicians, cooks and 'even of all kitchin-moveables, only the Chimney excepted'[72]). Marvell travelled with the Ambassador and their vessel reached the Russian port of Archangel in less than a month; the other ship suffered 'troubles and disasters' (p.23) and took twice as long.

We have a wonderfully detailed and lively account of this visit to Russia and Scandinavia, over which it would be a great temptation to linger for its narrative of a quite astonishing journey and its glimpses of the Russian kingdom. It was written by the under-secretary of the Embassy, Guy Miège, perhaps with help from Marvell, who was, as he had told the Mayor of Hull, the Secretary. Miège's *Relation* was published in English and French in 1669 and was designed to justify the conduct of the English delegation after the Russians had lodged, quite gratuitously, a formal complaint about it. Marvell's main task during the trip was to undertake general correspondence—several letters from Carlisle to Charles II have survived in Marvell's handwriting—to draft and read state documents, and generally to assist with his linguistic skills. He himself has told us nothing whatsoever about the trip; its excitements and frustrations must have made some impression upon him—indeed, we *do* know from Miège's *Relation* that he was brought near to losing his temper on several occasions and once, with his wagon driver near Hamburg on the return journey, actually did so:

The Secretary not able to bring him to reason by fair means, tried what he could do by foul, and by clapping a pistol to his head would have forced him along with him. But immediately his pistol was wrested from him, and as they were putting themselves into a posture to abuse him, we interposed so effectually, that he was rescued out of the hands of a barbarous rout of peasants and Mechanicks.

(pp.430-1)

The important Russian instalment of the long embassy ultimately proved a failure, since the Russians would not grant any of the trading privileges sought. Carlisle reported to Charles II that the Czar himself was 'of an excellent good humour, goodly pressence and agreeable discourse'. But unfortunately the Czar's commissioners, appointed to negotiate with the English, were quite otherwise, being arrogant, difficult and capricious. Again Carlisle reports (though one wonders if Marvell added any embellishments as he transcribed the letters): 'What else was to be expected in a country where all other beasts change their colours twice a yeare but the rationall beasts change their soules thrice a day'. The 'great rudeness and insolence of the Muscovites', in Miège's phrase (p.24), and the 'slownesse ... of those Sonns of Winter', in Carlisle's, were the main obstacles to a smooth and successful mission. Both were encountered first upon the Ambassador's setting foot upon Russian soil and one or other attended the English party throughout their stay; they proved, as the Ambassador noted, 'very troublesome and incorrigible in matters of Ceremony'.

We first read of Marvell on the occasion of the initial ceremony of the Ambassador's landing: 'in expectation of Orders for his Entry... he sent

Mr *Marvel* his Secretary into the Town. Of whose landing, the Governour having notice, ordered him to be conducted by six Gentlemen to the Castle, through a Regiment of six hundred men, and the next day he sent sixteen boats, guarded by several hundreds of men ... to receive his Excellence, and bring him ashore' (p.23). It was at that point that the official sent to convey Carlisle to his lodgings snubbed him, the first of many such calculated gestures of hauteur by the Czar's messengers.

From Archangel to Vologda the English party travelled on river barges, pulled by men, not horses. The logistics of this section of the journey were sometimes impossible, notably the cooking facilities on one barge having to supply the others that could not all get alongside. They amused themselves by shooting duck or by trying to outdrink the Governor of Tetmar (unsuccessfully). They kept warm along the rivers and on the sledges (plate 55) in the next stage of the journey from Vologda to Moscow by wrapping themselves in furs and imbibing 'strong waters' copiously (p.93). At Vologda they were delayed three months, partly by the weather and partly by the calculations of the Russians. But they hunted, danced—much to their hosts' amazement, but to the larger employment of those six musicians—celebrated Guy Fawkes' Night with 'artificial fire-works, made by an *Englishman* with great skill and success' (p.99), and enlarged their number by the birth of a son to the butler's wife. The journey onwards to Moscow was by sledge—sixty of which were sent as an advance party, with the main company on one hundred and forty sledges following. Marvell was involved here in an altercation over these sledges, which the Russians should have supplied, but would not:

my Lord Ambassador dispatched his Secretary to him, who told him freely it was most undecent to have persons of quality worse accommodated for their confidence in the Care of the *Tzar* so great a Monarch, than if they had been at their own charges. He replied they might do as they pleased, no body hindered them from takeing their own course. And thereupon he declared that his Excellence had no reason, to complain, that his *Tzarskoy* Majesty had done him extraordinary honor in sending a person of his quality so far to conduct him to *Mosco*. To which the Secretary replied, that my Lord Ambassador acknowledged his quality, but he never thought it so great, that he and his associate ought to prefer themselves before him as they had done at their first visit.   (p.105)

Marvell's 'free' speech and quick retorts obviously just managed to contain his violent irritation in diplomatic language.

They eventually reached Moscow, but were kept waiting for their state entry; although invited to be ready at an early hour and having even sent their kitchens ahead, they were kept without food and with no further word until the late evening. They started at last, but were still subjected to what Miège records as further 'misfortune, if not an indignity' (p.122). Carlisle retaliated by ordering his trumpeters not to sound. But he lost the

55 The winter travelling sledge of a Russian nobleman, by Erich Palmquist, 1674.

next round of diplomatic niceties, which centred upon the delicate matter of precedence in alighting from the sledges, when the '*Pronchissof* [the Czar's messenger] tooke occasion to deceive his Excellence, and falsify his word, hanging in the aire betwixt the armes of his servants, and but touching the earth with his tiptoes, whilst the Ambassador came out freely' (p.132). They eventually made their state entry into the city, reportedly one of the most splendid such events ever witnessed, and Marvell had a central position in the ceremonies:

In the Ambassadors sledg there was the Secretary and the chief Interpreter standing and uncovered, the Secretary carrying in his hands upon a yard of red Damaske his Letters of Credence written in parchment, whose Superscription contained all the titles of the Tzar in letters of Gold.   (p.146)

Difficulties arose almost immediately with the Latin address by Marvell to Czar Alexis, who chose to be offended at being greeted with '*Illustrissimus*' rather than with '*Serenissimus*'. And there was at least one further incident in which Marvell's Latinity allowed the Czar to pretend exasperation (pp.318–19). The diplomatic shuttlecock proceeded. Even Carlisle got angry on one occasion and, raising his voice at a meeting with the Commissioners, caused—according to their complaint—a casement window to fall into the room (p.191)! The sterile exchanges were interspersed with further ceremonies, at one of which (Carlisle reported to Charles II) the Czar 'asked how does the disconsolate widow of that Glorious Martyr King Charles the first'; there were football matches among the English, and Russian feasts, one of which on 19 February 1664 lasted nine hours and consisted of five hundred dishes. Marvell, as Legouis noticed[73], had to compose and deliver some harsh attacks upon his former friends and colleagues in the Commonwealth; these speeches were designed by Carlisle to mollify the Czar's still smouldering outrage at the regicide. Maybe as a consequence the Czar seems to have extended an especial honour to Marvell by presenting him with the head of a sturgeon, deemed a choice item, during that interminable February feast. Unsuccessful as they were in their main endeavour, the English party must have been glad to leave. Among their souvenirs Miège records two Russian bears (p.378).

The last stages of their journey took them to the Swedish and Danish courts, where standards of hospitality and courtesy were higher and more predictable than among the Muscovites. But neither diplomacy achieved anything of consequence, and the support of the Scandinavian countries in the second Dutch War (1665–7) was not forthcoming. Apart from his fight with the wagoner between Bockstoudt and Bremen, Marvell was involved in one less violent, more calculated, incident. At the Swedish Court, where Christina, flattered in the verses to Ingelo over ten years ago, had abdicated in 1654, it was Charles XI, aged nine, and the Queen Mother who listened to the addresses. On one such occasion Carlisle, 'about the middle of his Speech where he saith, *That the boldest Eloquence would lose its Speech*, his Excellence made a long pause, as if by that he designed to have verified what he had said'. Everybody was much affected by the apparent sincerity of the Ambassador, speechless at his high task. But when Marvell, reading the French version immediately afterwards, also paused in the same place, it was perceived to 'have been so contrived' (pp.373–4).

Marvell returned to play a more active role in and outside Parliament. He had left on the mission to Russia when it was still enjoying what today would be called 'a honeymoon period' with the restored King. In 1665, on his return, despite some general approval of the new Dutch War, there was increasing criticism of the King's ministers in general and of the persecution of Nonconformists in particular; Marvell evidently subscribed to those disaffections:

> Imperial prince, king of the seas and isles,
> Dear object of our joys and Heaven's smiles:
> What boots it that thy light does gild our days
> And we lie basking in thy milder rays,
> While swarms of insects, from thy warmth begun,
> Our land devour and intercept our sun?
> Thou, like Jove's Minos, rul'st a greater Crete
> And for its hundred cities count'st thy fleet.
> Why wilt thou that state-Daedalus allow,
> Who builds thee but a lab'rinth and a cow?

The lines are from a poem of 1666 for which Marvell has been held responsible. Clarendon, the chief policy-maker of the King, is alluded to

56 Battle of Lowestoft, engraving, 1665.

as Daedalus whose craft has erected a labyrinth for Charles and—so it has
been suggested—provided him with a cow of a barren queen (instead of
the Minotaur). Marvell's responsibility for this and related satires has
been argued fairly convincingly by George de F. Lord[74] and, though
doubts remain, it is useful to consider them as if by Marvell. They share,
after all, sufficient themes and techniques with such items as 'Clarindon's
House-Warming' [pp.143–6] and 'The last Instructions to a Painter'
[pp.147–71] which were admitted to the canon by Margoliouth. Even if
the doubtful poems are rejected, within two years at the latest of resuming
his parliamentary duties Marvell is sufficiently disturbed both by
government policies and by their uncritical poetical supporters to raise his
voice anonymously outside the House.

The whole sequence of poems we are to consider derive from an
effusion by Edmund Waller, 'Instructions to a Painter' of 1665. Waller
doubtless had to compensate in the new regime for the indiscreet verses
on Cromwell he had written earlier, so he chose the abortive victory of the
English fleet over the Dutch at Lowestoft on 3 June 1665 (plate 56) upon

which to write a panegyric. The structure of the poem is the writer's pretence that he is instructing a painter in how to represent the naval event:

> First draw the sea, that portion which between
> The greater world and this of ours is seen;
> Here place the British, there the Holland fleet,
> Vast floating armies, both prepared to meet!
> Draw the whole world expecting who shall reign,
> After this combat, o'er the conquered main.
> Make Heav'n concerned and an unusual star
> Declare th'importance of th'approaching war. (p.20)

Marine paintings of this sort were a popular form with the Dutch painters (see plates 56 and 58), and increasingly known in England. Verbal instructions to such painters were merely the extension of a popular Renaissance theory of the interchangeability of the arts *(ut pictura poesis)*[75]. Waller does not always keep the basic form in mind, and he has to apologize by the end:

> Painter, excuse me, if I have a while
> Forgot thy art and used another style,
> For, though you draw armed heroes as they sit,
> The task in battle does the Muses fit. (p.28)

This gives Marvell or the author of 'The Second Advice to a Painter' the chance to contribute a fuller and far less flattering picture of the first year of the Dutch War:

> Nay, Painter, if thou dar'st design that fight
> Which Waller only courage had to write,
> If thy bold hand can, without shaking, draw
> What e'en the actors trembled when they saw
> (Enough to make thy colors change like theirs
> And all thy pencils bristle like their hairs)
> First, in fit distance of the prospect main,
> Paint... (p.32)

Waller's unqualified praise had excluded various unfavourable details of the Battle of Lowestoft, which the second writer delightedly supplies: 'Paint Allin tilting at the coast of Spain:/Heroic act, and never heard till now'. The satirist chooses to paint a larger section of naval history, beginning with the inept voyage of Sir Thomas Allin, two of whose ships ran aground in the Straits of Gibraltar, and he also emphasizes the greedy motives of those involved ('But Coventry sells the whole fleet away'). Unlike Waller, who discourses at length upon the bravery of the English commanders, 'Marvell' (it will be aptest to signify the author of the disputed poems in this way) sees the whole war characterized by cowardice and incompetence—to such an extent that even Neptune is disturbed ('Draw pensive Neptune, biting of his thumbs,/To think himself a slave whos'e'er o'ercomes'). Typical of these ironic adjustments of perspective and colouring is his account of the incident when the English fleet put into Harwich to revictual, having sailed up and down the Dutch coast for ten days without attacking the enemy ships, which promptly emerged once the English had left. Waller celebrates the return to port and the visit of the Duchess of York thus:

> But who can always on the billows lie?
> The wat'ry wilderness yields no supply:
> Spreading our sails, to Harwich we resort,
> And meet the beauties of the British court.
> Th'illustrious duchess and her glorious train
> (Like Thetis with her nymphs) adorn the main.
> The gazing sea-gods, since the Paphian queen
> Sprung from among them, no such sight had seen.
> Charmed with the graces of a troop so fair,
> These deathless powers for us themselves declare,
> Resolved the aid of Neptune's court to bring
> And help the nation where such beauties spring.
> The soldier here his wasted store supplies
> And takes new valor from the ladies' eyes.
>   Meanwhile, like bees, when stormy winter's gone,
> The Dutch (as if the sea were all their own)
> Desert their ports, and, falling in their way,
> Our Hamburg merchants are become their prey...   (p.23)

The satirist ridicules both the accuracy of the narrative and the propriety of its poetic decoration: the English

> Hedge the Dutch in only to let them out.
> So huntsmen fair unto the hares give law,
> First find them and then civilly withdraw;
>
> . . .
>   But, Painter, now prepare, t'enrich thy piece,
> Pencil of ermines, oil of ambergris:
> See where the duchess, with triumphant tail
> Of num'rous coaches, Harwich does assail!
> So the land crabs, at Nature's kindly call,
> Down to engender at the sea do crawl.
> See then the admiral, with navy whole,
> To Harwich through the ocean caracole.   (p.34)

The verse is more jaunty, less ceremonial and poly-syllabled than

Waller's; it exploits absurdities with strained similes and mythological conceits; roles are wickedly reversed—the flamboyant naval imagery of the Duchess's attack upon Harwich contrasts with the English failure to press their advantage against the Dutch ports; the verse even manages to parade its own irregularities and awkwardnesses, notably inept rhythms and bathetic rhymes, as typical of what it describes, as 'natural' as the animal instincts which take precedence over military considerations. The poet's annoyance at sheer incompetence flashes savagely once or twice—'His shattered head the fearless duke distains/And gave the last-first proof that he had brains' (p.38).

The anger of 'Marvell' is most ferocious in its denunciation, put into the mouth of a sailor, of 'damned and treble damned' Clarendon:

> Who, to divert the danger of the war
> With Bristol, hounds us on the Hollander;
> Fool-coated gownman! sells, to fight with Hans,
> Dunkirk; dismantling Scotland, quarrels France;
> And hopes he now hath bus'ness shaped and power
> T' outlast his life or ours and 'scape the Tower;
> And that he yet may see, ere he go down,
> His dear Clarinda circled in a crown.   (p.37)

Such passages now need a commentary, but once elucidated, the contemptuous ferocity of the attack on Clarendon is seen to be firmly premised in the victim's own actions, which emerged unscathed when the Earl of Bristol sought to impeach Clarendon in the Lords. 'Marvell' glances at the sale of Dunkirk to the French, the dismantling of Scottish forts that Cromwell had built, the refusal of French help in mediating between Holland and England, and the ambitious marriage of his daughter to the Duke of York, heir to the throne. It is obviously the incompetence at home and at sea that distresses the poet rather than the war itself. Marvell's 'Character of Holland' was reissued in 1665, probably without his permission, though equally probably without dismaying him. The contrast which the 'Second Advice' implies between Cromwell's Dutch War, celebrated in the earlier poem, and the dereliction of the Commonwealth ideal ('The Ocean is the Fountain of Command', I.118) are the central and final complaints:

> Thus having fought we know not why, as yet,
> We've done we know not what nor what we get.   (p.42)

The King, however, is excluded from censure in a passage already quoted (above, p.148). In this the poet concurred with Parliament, which, although it investigated and expelled one of its members, Henry Brouncker, who ordered the fleet not to pursue the Dutch after the Battle of Lowestoft, nevertheless voted the King vast sums of money to continue the war. Marvell attended this session, held at Oxford since the plague was raging in London during October 1665. But he must have resented the price paid for the Commons' generosity, which involved increasingly severe measures against Nonconformists, all designed to exclude them from any share in local or central government (the Act of Uniformity, 1662; Conventicle Act, 1664; Five Mile Act, 1665).

The war, despite a re-shuffle of the high command, continued as sadly as before, and off Dunkirk in June 1666 a divided English fleet was badly mauled by the Dutch. Parliament investigated the incident over a year afterwards, but meanwhile the anonymous satirist struck again with 'The Third Advice to a Painter', which appeared early in 1667—Pepys records seeing it in manuscript as early as January[76]. It employs the same conventions and tactics as before, though its more scurrilous and smutty tone is indicated by its initial choice of painter:

> Sandwich in Spain now, and the duke in love,
> Let's with new gen'rals a new painter prove:
> Lely's a Dutchman, danger in his art;
> His pencils may intelligence impart.
> Thou, Gibson, that among thy navy small
> Of marshalled shells commandest admiral
> (Thyself so slender that thou show'st no more
> Than barnacle new-hatched of them before)
> Come, mix thy water-colours and express,
> Drawing in little, how we do yet less. (p.46)

Richard Gibson was a dwarf who painted miniatures, an apt form, the poet implies, for England's diminished sea-power. The tone and structure also confirm the diminution from Lely to Gibson, oil to water-colour: the jokes are in poor taste—much capital being made of the incident when 'His Grace's bum' was partly shot away—and a large part of the poem given over as a speech to the Duchess of Albemarle, wife of the new joint naval commander, General Monck, now created a Duke. Thus 'Marvell' not only really abandons the format of instructing a painter, but introduces the spirited invective of this 'Presbyterian sibyl' to do his work for him. She fulminates against everything that seems to hamper her husband's enterprise, suggesting that it is Clarendon who conspires to disgrace the man who had acted so loyally for Charles II at his Restoration. 'Marvell' also manages to let her Presbyterian rage hit at the return of bishops to the House of Lords and the expulsion of Nonconformists from their churches by the Act of Uniformity. The poet's final address continues to exclude the King from the strictures against his ministers:

> What servants will conceal and couns'lers spare
> To tell, the painter and the poet dare. (p.58)

He voices, too, the sentiment widely held at the time that the Great Fire of London, which began in September 1666, was the expiation of England's sins (p.51).

Marvell only mentions the Fire subsequently in a letter to Lord Wharton: 'I see they are staking out the City every day but can observe litle hast of building. Somebody told me yesterday that a merry or a simple fellow was looking on, and misliking somewhat in their laying out of the streets, said Poh, if they do it no better then thus, the City had as good never have bin burn't' [II.310–11]. That he felt the same way about the government is clear from the satire with which Marvell *is* credited, 'The Last Instructions to a Painter'. Earlier examples of 'Cassandra's song', whether by Marvell or not, had seemed ineffective and he rolls his political strength into one 'Last' indictment[77].

The canvas of the poem is vast, like some burlesque equivalent of Rubens's Whitehall ceiling. It is crowded with satiric portraits, with a parliamentary narrative of quite astonishing scope and accurate detail, with large naval vistas; this visual repertoire joins with an equally versatile range of verbal irony and invective to justify the poet's own claim for this collaborative enterprise:

> Where pencil cannot, there my pen shall do't
> ...
> How well our arts agree
> Poetic picture, painted poetry.

The poem gains above all from its remarkable fidelity to historical facts. Indeed, George de F. Lord claims that 'No other Restoration poem is more comprehensive or specific in its treatment of public affairs. Not even the ubiquitous and omniscient Pepys is so accurate in recording the events of this crucial last year of the war' (p.66). This realism of Marvell's, though, should hardly surprise us, for he has always had his eye firmly on the factual, literal, or topographical, even as he negotiates the conceits and surprises of mental territory.

Yet the density of contemporary allusion emerges with an instant and engaging satiric existence, which is (initially at least) independent of the need for annotation. Marvell's lengthy vision of his own parliamentary colleagues, drawn up in mimic armies that parody the larger conflicts of the Dutch War, has an immediate impact. The 'Gross bodies, grosser minds, and grossest cheats', for instance, of the Court party—

> Sir Fred'rick and Sir Saloman draw lots
> For the command of politics or sots,

> Thence fall to words, but, quarrel to adjourn,
> Their friends agreed they should command by turn.
> Cart'ret the rich did the accountants guide
> And in ill English all the world defied.
> The Papists—but of these the House had none;
> Else Talbot offered to have led them on.
> Bold Duncombe next, of the projectors chief,
> And old Fitzhardinge of the Eaters Beet.
> Late and disordered, out the drinkers drew;
> Scarce them their leaders, they their leaders knew.
> Before them entered, equal in command,
> Apsley and Brod'rick, marching hand in hand.
> Last then but one, Powell, that could not ride,
> Led the French standard, welt'ring in his stride.
> He, to excuse his slowness, truth confessed
> That 'twas so long before he could be dressed.
> The lords' sons, last, all these did reinforce:
> Cornb'ry before them managed hobby-horse.

The innuendoes in a passage like that are made explicit with a malicious and energetic relish in some of the longer set-piece portraits, among the best of which is certainly that of Lady Castlemaine, famed for her innumerable *amours*:

> Paint Castlemaine in colours that will hold
> (Her, not her picture, for she now grows old):
> She through her lackey's drawers, as he ran,
> Discerned love's cause and a new flame began.
> Her wonted joys thenceforth and court she shuns,
> And still within her mind the footman runs:
> His brazen calves, his brawny thighs (the face
> She slights), his feet shaped for a smoother race.
> Poring within her glass she readjusts
> Her looks and oft-tried beauty now distrusts;
> Fears lest he scorn a woman once assayed,
> And now first wished she e'er had been a maid.
> Great Love, how dost thou triumph and how reign,
> That to a groom could'st humble her disdain!
> Stripped to her skin, see how she stooping stands,
> Nor scorns to rub him down with those fair hands,
> And washing (lest the scent her crime disclose)
> His sweaty hooves, tickles him 'twixt the toes.

But the poem does not—cannot, really, over nearly one thousand lines—rely simply upon such satiric portraits. They are used to enliven and sustain two long and connected narratives, one parliamentary, one naval, by which Marvell focuses his case against the royal advisors and the

Court party. Both narratives and portraits alike are shaped by Marvell's characteristically double vision: panegyric and lampoon, heroic and ignominious, great and small, important and trivial, all coexist and are ultimately inseparable. It is the strategy of which he speaks in *The Rehearsal Transpros'd*, 'making the same thing serve for a Panegyrick or a Philippick' (p.24).

The poem begins with a microscope and ends with a telescope. The latter enables man to discover the spots on the sun. The former, in Robert Hooke's *Micrographia* (1655), studies the under-belly of a louse clinging to a human hair (plate 57). The poem is therefore contained within two up-to-date scientific images, which establish and authorize the poet's realism. Yet they also endorse his distortions. In the meadows at Nun Appleton he had once studied the preternatural aspect of small things made great ('such Fleas, ere they approach the Eye,/In Multiplying Glasses lye') and great made small ('as we walk more low than' grasshoppers). And later, Swift was to expose Gulliver to a political education by alternative disproportions. So Marvell in 'Last Instructions' requires his painter to attend to a world where their joint perspective enlarges and miniaturizes. The comptroller of the household, Lord Clifford, viewed in the light of Hooke's *Micrographia*, suddenly becomes 'a tall louse brandish[ing] the white staff', ridiculously small. (Thus Marvell pays Clifford back for that incident in 1662, when after their quarrel in the Commons he was forced to confess that he'd 'given the first Provocation' and to apologize[78].) Yet the under-belly of a louse, though small, can be made grotesquely large under the scientist's or the satirist's microscope. St Albans, the English Ambassador at the French Court, is first reduced to 'soup and gold' and belittled by his lust. Trivial as this last is in comparison with what he should display, it is nevertheless vastly impressive:

> He needs no seal but to St James's lease,
> Whose breeches were the instruments of peace;
> Who, if the French dispute his pow'r, from thence
> Can straight produce them a plenipotence.

Lackey or hero have eventually the same size and shape in Lady Castlemaine's eyes, though the one is first aggrandized, the other reduced. The satirist views these animals, a collection of curiosities, with the passionate regard of the virtuosi, whose cabinets he must have seen across Europe as well as in Yorkshire; like Francis Bacon, he 'never studied nature more'.

The interchange of great and small continues through the long and obviously first-hand account of Parliament's debates over the excise, which for effect are foreshortened. The M.P.s play their war-games with enthusiasm:

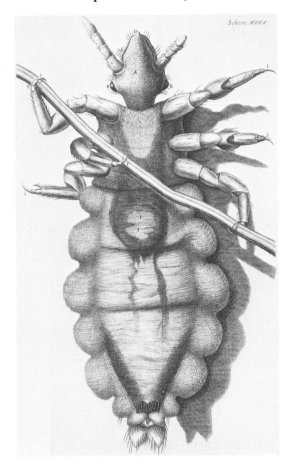

57 Louse under the microscope, engraving from R. Hooke's *Micrographia*, 1665.

> They both accept the charge with merry glee,
> To fight a battle from all gunshot free.
> Pleased with their numbers, yet in valour wise,
> They feign a parley, better to surprise:
> They that ere long shall the rude Dutch upbraid,
> Who in a time of treaty durst invade.

But the larger and 'realer' war against the Dutch which continues elsewhere puts into perspective their playing 'with small acts the public game'. Yet while their skirmishes may have the miniature effects of fairy-tale—

58　*Dutch Ships in the Medway June 1667*, by Jan Peters.

> Such once Orlando, famous in romance,
> Broached whole brigades like larks upon his lance

—what Parliament is, after all, debating is the large and hideous prospect of

> Excise, a monster worse than e'er before
> Frighted the midwife and the mother tore.
> A thousand hands she has and thousand eyes,
> Breaks into shops and into cellars pries,
> With hundred rows of teeth the shark exceeds,
> And on all trade like cassowar she feeds:
> Chops off the piece where'er she close the jaw,
> Else swallows all down her indented maw.

A similar sense of schoolboy squabbles minimizes the actual war, as St Albans tries to pretend with Louis XIV that 'the Hollanders do make a noise,/Threaten to beat us, and are naughty boys'.

The serious and humiliating incident of 10–15 June 1667, when the

Dutch navy sailed up the Thames and Medway to Chatham, destroying and capturing English ships (plate 58), is also satirically prettified:

> Aeolus their sails inspires with eastern wind,
> Puffs them along, and breathes upon them kind.
> With pearly shell the Tritons all the while
> Sound the sea-march and guide to Sheppey Isle.

Some Ovidian colour is used, as well as distinct echoes of Enobarbus's

59   *Sea Triumph of Charles II*, by Antonio Verrio, 1670s.

narrative of Cleopatra's first seductive encounter with Antony, to make
the national disaster ironically gay and airy. But in keeping with the
painterly metaphor Marvell also invokes the bravura machinery of
baroque allegories (plate 59), the large theatrical confidence of which
scarcely matches the events. The visual language that Rubens (mentioned
at line 119) and his English imitators employed for state occasions only
underlines the lack of a true British occasion when it is imitated by
Marvell. Michael de Ruyter's, the Dutch Admiral's,

> sporting navy all about him swim
> And witness their complacence in their trim.
> Their streaming silks play through the weather fair
> And with inveigling colours court the air,
> While the red flags breathe on their top-masts high
> Terror and war but want an enemy.
> Among the shrouds the seamen sit and sing,
> And wanton boys on every rope do cling
> . . .
> So have I seen in April's bud arise
> A fleet of clouds, sailing along the skies;
> The liquid region with their squadrons filled,
> Their airy sterns the sun behind does gild,
> And gentle gales them steer, and Heaven drives,
> With thunder and lightning from each armed cloud...

The spectacle of the Dutch in the Medway becomes, in another iron-
ical adjudication of its significance, simply a 'new play', with 'feathered
gallants' lining the shore like the beau-monde at a theatre. (Marvell seems
to use the contemporary theatre, so popular with King and Court, as a
measure of the unstrenuous times—see below, p.179). Yet on this
occasion, though the gallants probably do not appreciate it, the tragedy
they view is the real one of Archibald Douglas, who died defending the
Royal Oak, fired by the Dutch. His brave example—celebrated elsewhere
by Marvell in 'The Loyall Scot' [pp.180–7]—is presented as if it were some
Restoration heroic tragedy, the hero of which is classically brave and
modishly libertine:

> Like a glad lover the fierce flames he meets
> And tries his first embraces in their sheets.
> . . .
> And, as on angels' heads their glories shine,
> His burning locks adorn his face divine.
> But when in his immortal mind he felt
> His alt'ring form and soldered limbs to melt,
> Down on the deck he laid himself and died,
> With his dear sword reposing by his side

60 *Nell Gwyn*, artist unknown, 1670s (?).

> And on the flaming plank so rests his head
> As one that's warmed himself and gone to bed.

Thus handled, Douglas's courage seems both magnificent and rather ridiculous or at least sentimental, like the affected Restoration lover. Marvell invokes various languages of art: those of the theatre, romance, baroque allegory (plate 59), even numismatics ('The Court in farthing'—perhaps a reference to the Naval Victories Medal of 1667,

161

where Britannia was modelled by one of Charles II's sweethearts). Such languages all serve the satirist as distorting glasses, enlarging and diminishing the brute instincts of the times ('our great debauch and little skills'). A final example wickedly involves the King himself. He first mistakes a naked apparition for some *décolletée* Nell Gwyn (plate 60), thus losing the sublimity of his midnight vision; but his belated and 'deep thoughts' register that it was an allegorical figure of 'England or the Peace', and a new seriousness emerges from the *risqué* picture.

The basic argument is still the same as that employed by 'Marvell' in the two earlier 'Advices', and the final address 'To the King' continues to exclude him from the condemnation of his vicious or foolish servants. However, a considerable satiric imagination has inevitably complicated the clear outlines of good and bad, so that the final lines must work to clarify the political message. Significantly, they do this by reversing the conflating manoeuvres of the poem and by pointing out the false distinctions and divisions that contemporary politics have contrived:

> Bold and accursed are they that all this while
> Have strove to isle our monarch from his isle,
> And to improve themselves, on false pretense,
> About the common prince have raised a fence;
> The kingdom from the crown distinct would see
> And peel the bark to burn at last the tree.
> But Ceres corn, and Flora is the spring,
> Bacchus is wine, the country is the king.

It has been argued that this final line also equates the King's integrity with the Country, as opposed to the Court, party in Parliament[79]. By the time 'Last Instructions' was finished, some time before Clarendon's flight to France in November 1667, Marvell had identified himself clearly with the opposition. He had been involved closely with all the parliamentary events of his poem, having been one of those 'citizens and merchants' whom he represents among the victorious army against Excise. We know that he spoke against the sailors' being 'paid' with tickets, and against the committal of Peter Pett to the Tower—'Last Instructions' mocks all those who tried to make a scapegoat of this superintendent of the Chatham dockyard. And, despite some odd reports of his actual speeches in the Commons, Marvell also joined those who worked for the overthrow of Clarendon, identifying himself at least over this matter with the heterogeneous opposition gathered around the Duke of Buckingham, husband of his former pupil, Mary Fairfax.

We know something of where and how Marvell figures in the 'Landskip of our Mottly Parliament' [p.176] from the diary kept by another member, John Milward, between September 1666 and May 1668. In it he noted brief details of a debate of 14 October 1667 on Clarendon's conduct:

This morning was wholly spent in speeches concerning the Lord Chancellor, whether the King's laying him aside should be joined to the other acts of grace for which we were to give him the thanks of the House; many excellent speeches were made against it by Sir Robert Atkins, Sir John Maynard, Mr Marvell. . . intimating that it was a precondemning him before any crime was laid to his charge.

(ed. cit., p.86)

It's a puzzling entry about a man who otherwise was against Clarendon. Perhaps, as the editor of Milward's diary has suggested, he sought to prevent the opponents of the Chancellor from forming another Court faction; perhaps he was merely trying to get Clarendon's impeachment on a firm legal basis, which his letters to Hull of 23 and 26 November [II.61] imply was his concern; perhaps, as Caroline Robbins also suggested, he was 'constantly in opposition'. Another report of presumably the same speech, printed in an appendix to *The Diary of John Milward* (p.328), does not, unfortunately, enlighten us much more:

The raising and destroying of favourites and creatures is the sport of kings not to be meddled with by us. Kings in the choice of their ministers move in a sphere distinct from us. It is said because the people rejoiced at his fall we must thank the King. The people also rejoiced at the restoration of the Duke of Buckingham the other day obnoxious. Shall we not thank the King for that too? It is said we hate him not. Would any man in this House be willing to have such a vote pass upon him?

One further explanation is that Marvell, despite his opposition to Clarendon, against whom the temper of the times was likely to prevail anyway, delighted to explore arguments inside the House under his own name which outside in anonymous satires he could prosecute more freely and without concern for the legal procedures. In his role as Member, he even suggests in a letter to Hull of 14 November that Clarendon's impeachment is taking time away from other important business [II.59].

Outside the House, 'CLARINDON's House-Warming' and two other squibs he'd written [I.143-7] were circulating in print or manuscript by the late summer of 1667. There were, of course, sides of the Lord Chancellor that Marvell ignored or could not yet have known about—including his authorship of *The History of the Rebellion and Civil Wars in England*; though, with fine and larger historical irony, it was only Clarendon's banishment that provided him with the opportunity to bring that magnificent work to completion. What preoccupied Marvell in 1667 was the Chancellor's responsibility for the government's chicanery and ineptitude. His newly built mansion near St James offered itself to the poet as to the London mob as an apt symbol; it was not only built out of stones purchased from St Paul's, though designed for repairs to that cathedral, but also—more figuratively—built at England's larger expense:

Upon his House

Here lies the sacred Bones
Of *Paul* late gelded of his Stones.
Here lie Golden Briberies,
The price of ruin'd Families:
The Cavaliers Debenter-Wall,
Fixt on an Eccentrick Basis;
Here's *Dunkirk-Town* and *Tangier-Hall*,
The Queens Marriage and all;
The Dutchman's *Templum Pacis.*

The longer poem elaborates these pithy and gnomic charges into a looser, explicit invective; perhaps Marvell even chose to ape the style of popular broadsides. Clarendon's turning architect in time of plague, war and fire ('three Deluges threatning our Land') becomes the final insult added to the injuries of humiliation by the Dutch navy (for which Clarendon became the scapegoat) and of his hostility to Parliament (associated in the popular mind with his advocacy of standing armies).

'The Last Instructions', taking a more considered survey of events, also connects Clarendon with what Marvell saw, with some prescience, as a complacent alliance with the French. St Albans acted as the Chancellor's messenger-boy to Louis XIV. Marvell specifically warns the King, since he seemed oblivious, of the noise that 'the Drums Lewis's March did beat', a reference to French designs upon Flanders and, more generally, to the manifest untrustworthiness of France as a mediator between the English and the Dutch. Earlier in the poem the Court party had marched under a 'French standard' in the excise battle—a happy pun, since it links a dangerous political alliance with France to the syphilitic consequences of other Court *ententes* ('our great debauch and little skills'). The larger wisdom of these anti-French analyses in 'Last Instructions' may be the result of its longer meditation and revision in the light of developing events. A reworking of the poem is even perhaps hinted at in the lines that claim 'To paint or write/Is longer work and harder than to fight'. It was not published in an acknowledged form until after Marvell's death; but it did appear, maybe as early as 1669, in an anonymous tract together with 'The Loyall Scot'; it was probably too long to have circulated in manuscript copies.

With Clarendon's escape to France, this phase of Marvell's extra-parliamentary life comes to an end. When the Commons heard of his flight they requested 'that care might be taken for Securing all the Sea-Ports lest he should pass there'; Marvell's letter to the Mayor adds that 'I suppose he will not trouble you at Hull' [II.63]. Marvell continues to keep his constituents informed on such parliamentary affairs as the inquiries into the 'miscarriages of the late warre' [p.65]. There are also glimpses of his private pursuits—when Parliament had met at Oxford during the plague in 1665 he took the opportunity to visit Bodley's Library, while two years later he tells a friend, Sir John Trott, 'The Word of God: The Society of good men: and the books of the Ancients' [pp.312–13] are the comforts and strengths of life. And he keeps up with at least some of the ephemeral journalism, reporting on it to William Popple in Bordeaux. He also seems to have developed an obsession with fires; he hears of outbreaks in Hull and urges vigilance upon the Mayor, but then adds that 'We have had so much of them here in the South that it makes me almost superstitious' [p.55]. But generally, the end of the Dutch War, the flight of Clarendon and the Triple Alliance signed between England, Sweden and Holland in 1668 seem to have augured well. Just as London's rebuilding was afoot, so 'there never appeared a fairer season for men to obtain what their own hearts could wish either as to redresse of any former grievances or the constituting of good order and justice for the future' [p.57].

9 So peculiar and entertaining a conduct

The future was not to be as beneficent as Marvell anticipated. Between 1668 and 1672 he engaged in few literary and political activities outside his parliamentary duties. But events were maturing that would bring him back into the public eye—indeed, into the King's—in a manner he had never yet experienced, for *The Rehearsal Transpros'd* of 1672 was a huge success. Its publication made him, according to Bishop Burnet,

the liveliest droll of the age, who writ in a burlesque strain, but with so peculiar and entertaining a conduct, that from the king down to the tradesman his book was read with great pleasure. That not only humbled Parker, but the whole party: for the author of the Rehearsal Transprosed had all the men of wit (or, as the French phrase it, all the *laughers*) of his side[80].

The circumstances which promoted Marvell's new literary activity are complicated, their parliamentary aspect being what Pepys called 'a beast not to be understood'[81]. The ostensible object of his animadversions was the general persecution of Nonconformists and, in particular, the support given to such measures by Samuel Parker in various writings beginning with *A Discourse of Ecclesiastical Politie* of 1670. But the Anglican fervour against dissenters had become entangled in Charles II's domestic and especially foreign policies; to secure sufficient funds for his various projects the King was obliged to bargain with Parliament, which demanded in return increasingly strict measures against Nonconformists. Marvell summed up the disgraceful bargaining in one of his private letters to his nephew, Popple, in 1670:

The terrible Bill against Conventicles is sent up to the Lords... They are making mighty Alterations in the Conventicle Bill, (which, as we sent up, is the Quintessence of arbitrary Malice,) and sit whole Days, and yet proceed but by Inches, and will, at the End, probably affix a *Scotch* Clause of the King's Power in Externals. So the Fate of the Bill is uncertain, but must probably pass, being the Price of Money.   [II.314–15]

But what the Lords proposed, to restore the King's 'eclesiastical Prerogatives' [II.317], would have been just another 'Piece of absolute universal Tyranny'. A year later in another private letter to a Thomas Rolt, later President of the East India Company and a connection of Cromwell's, then in Persia, Marvell recounts the King's demand for 'three hundred thousand Pounds for his Navy...and that the Parliament should pay his Debts...which I hear are at this Day risen to four Millions'. His horror at this unaccountable extravagance is matched only by his alarm at the 'constant Courtiers, increased by the Apostate Patriots, who were bought off, for that Turn, some at six, others ten, one at fifteen, thousand Pounds in Mony, besides what offices, Lands, and Reversions, to others, that it is a Mercy they gave not away the whole Land, and Liberty, of *England*' [II.324–5]. But within a year he was given an opportunity of loyally supporting the King *and* declaring against Anglican intolerance. Even so it was not to be a simple matter of commitment.

By a secret agreement with the French in 1670 (the Treaty of Dover) Charles II had accepted French subsidies, thus relieving him in part from the need to beg from Parliament; in return he agreed he would attack Holland and, when the time was ripe, declare himself a Roman Catholic. Yet the Triple Alliance was still in force, and the English Parliament continuing to pay for naval preparations against France. In 1672, more confident for a while because of the funds from Louis XIV, Charles issued a Declaration of Indulgence for Catholics and Dissenters and two days later, on 17 March, declared war on Holland. The first action was the more problematical, for in asserting a monarch's powers to dispense religion Charles thereby encroached upon what Parliament took to be its rights. Marvell must therefore have been placed in something of a

61 Page from *The Rehearsal Transpros'd*, 1672, John Aubrey's copy showing his only annotation.

dilemma over the Declaration, while his suspicions of a French connection, as injurious in the long run to Protestantism at home, must have made him distrustful of the third Dutch War. He chose to support the domestic issue of toleration, a cause he had always espoused; but he appears actually to have voted against the Declaration[82], and it certainly gets only a brief if nonetheless approving mention in *The Rehearsal Transpros'd* [p.73]. If the record of his vote is correct, I suspect it may be yet another instance of his antithetical nature. He had confessed to his nephew that as Members of Parliament 'We are venal Cowards' and asked 'what Probability is there of my doing any Thing to the Purpose?' [II.317 and 315]. Yet outside the House he could choose his own tactics and define his own territory, for 'in this World a good Cause signifies little, unless it be as well defended' [p.324]. Recalling the advice of his Spanish fencing instructor, he offered—if not the first blow—an attack that was better than a defence.

The Rehearsal Transpros'd took its title from a contemporary play by the Duke of Buckingham, *The Rehearsal*, which had received its first performance on 7 December 1671. In it a character called Bayes (who satirically represents Dryden) describes how he writes:

I take a book in my hand, either at home, or elsewhere, for that's all one, if there be any Wit in't, as there is no Book but has some, I Transverse it; that is, if it be Prose put it into Verse, (but that takes up some time), if it be Verse, put it into Prose.

To which another character replies, 'Methinks, Mr *Bayes*, that putting Verse into Prose should be call'd Transprosing'. Bayes's account of his methods of composition suggests something of Marvell's approach to Parker's writings. Taking them up one by one, he extracts their curious 'wit' and subjects it to his own analysis, 'transprosing' its absurdities, portentousness and 'enthusiasm' into his own mixture of shrewd burlesque and agile intelligence. Thus:

For as to mens private Consciences he hath made them very inconsiderable, and, reading what he saith of them with some attention, I only found this new and important Discovery and great Priviledge of Christian Liberty, that *Thought is free*. We are however obliged to him for that, seeing by consequence we may think of him what we please.   [p.52]

It is difficult to convey in extracts the energetic vigour of this work, which advances in long paragraphs, flexible, exuberant, apparently seduced into conversational asides and parentheses which yet reveal themselves as ineluctably central to his argument.

Parker, Marvell's opponent, was a young Anglican divine, Archdeacon of Canterbury, holder of various parish livings, but (as Marvell delights to remind him in the second part of *The Rehearsal Transpros'd*, p.180ff.) a former Presbyterian and member of an Oxford group which 'used to Fast and Pray weekly together, but for their refection fed sometimes on a Broth from whence they were commonly call'd *Grewellers*'. He changed his beliefs after the Restoration and much 'Horoscoping up and down': 'And after having many times cast a figure, he at last satisfyed himself that the Episcopal Government would indure as long as this King lived, and from thence forward cast about how to be admitted into the Church of *England*, and find the Highway to her preferments'. These personal passages only came into the second part after Parker had counter-attacked by abusing Marvell personally. The first part turns its agile satire upon two aspects of Parker's writings: his authoritarian notion of government, derived largely from Hobbes, and especially his view of how matters of faith were to be controlled; his style and expression, which are intimately linked—Marvell had explored the same connection with Tom May—with his ideology. Marvell tackles three of Parker's works, one by one, for 'there being no method at all in his wild rambling talk; I must either tread just on in his footsteps, or else I shall be in a perpetual maze' [p.74]. The three writings are, first, *A Discourse of Ecclesiastical Politie, wherein the authority of the Civil Magistrate over the Consciences of Subjects in matters of Religion is asserted; the Mischiefs and Inconveniences of Toleration are represented, and all Pretences pleaded in behalf of Liberty of Conscience are fully answered* (1669), a title which fully declares its argument; next, *A Defence and Continuation of the Ecclesiastical Politie* (1671), which violently sought to answer John Owen's *Truth and Innocence Vindicated*, which had argued that matters of conscience were not to be controlled by civil powers; Parker's third piece, which finally provoked Marvell into writing, was *A Preface Shewing what grounds there are of Fears and Jealousies of Popery*, prefixed to Bishop Bramhall's *Vindication of himself and the Episcopal Clergy from the Presbyterian Charge of Popery* (1672). Such titles do not augur very exciting material, but it was Marvell's astonishing achievement to 'transverse' solemn and often stodgy disputations into buoyant and lively matter. 'And how he manages it', to use Marvell's own words on Parker, 'I had rather any man would learn by reading...than that I should be thought to misrepresent him, which I might, unless I transcribed the whole'. Nevertheless, some points can be made in *retail* if not in *wholesale*.

Whether in matters of principle or expression, it is Marvell's essential humanity that emerges and triumphs over Parker's 'spight against the Non-conformists' [p.104] and the 'presumption and arrogence of his stile' [p.143]:

That which astonishes me, and only raises my indignation is, that of all sorts of Men, this kind of Clergy should always be, and have been for the most precipitate, brutish, and sanguinary Counsels. The former Civil War cannot make them wise, nor his Majesties Happy Return, good natured... You would think the same day that they took up Divinity they divested themselves of Humanity... [pp.106–7]

Marvell may be vigorous in his mockery, quick to take an advantage with some stinging rebuke ('His Majesty may lay by his *Dieu* and use onely of his *Mon Droit*, p.65); but he emerges frequently from his ironies to make his own position clear, accusing Parker in the second paragraph of being indifferent to 'the business either of Truth or Eternity', of showing 'too slight an Apprehension and Knowledge of the duty we owe to our Saviour' [p.144] and of omitting, in his obsessive hatred of Nonconformity, any consideration of 'how we might live well with our Protestant Neighbours' [p.16]. His whole case against Parker's ideas and mode of writing is that 'though it hath been long practised, I never observed any great success by reviling man into *Conformity*' [p.36]. With one withering sentence he expresses his obligation to Parker 'for having proved that Nonconformity is the Sin against the Holy Ghost' [p.91].

Marvell's own religious preferences for prayer—the personal and spiritual dimension of a man's faith—over liturgy and outward shows inspire some engaging, if prejudiced, satire:

Candles, Crucifixes, Paintings, Images, Copes, bowing to the East, bowing to the Altar, and so many several Cringes & Genuflexions, that a man unpractised stood in need to entertain both a Dancing Master and a Remembrancer.

But in the next sentence he moves quickly from such matters, 'very uncouth to *English* Protestants, who naturally affect a plainness of fashion', to accept that if they had not been 'imposed and prest upon others' they would have been 'excusable' [pp.131–2]. It is this flexibility in writing, which matches his tolerance in religion, that makes Marvell's prose so readable. Manoeuvreability is also essential to his rapid shift backwards and forwards between seriousness and ridicule, which he himself identifies as his method [pp.49 and 187]. For, despite Burnet's description of *The Rehearsal Transpros'd* as burlesque, Marvell recognizes fundamentally serious issues. His contribution to literary modes of controversy was his recognition, equally, that serious matters matter at all levels—an insight that Swift's *A Tale of the Tub* and Pope's *Dunciad* were both to make especially their own and not without acknowledgement to Marvell's example[83]. Thus, he invokes instead of the Bible and theological authorities (thank heavens, the modern reader would say) many secular events, like Buckingham's play from which he took his title and the name of 'Bayes' that he saddles on Parker, or the whole world of Grub Street [pp.4–5]. From this contemporary journalism he derives both his use of details, for 'I am so subject to be particular' [II.353], and his popular imagery. Thus Parker's unscrupulous use of the dead Bramhall's *Vindication* for his own purposes is to make 'a constant Pissing-place of his grave' [p.28]; and later, ' though there was a Sow in *Arcadia* so fat and insensible that she suffered a Rats nest in her buttock, and they had both Dyet and Lodging in the same Gammon; yet it is not every *Rats* good fortune to be so well provided' [p.37].

As with such scurrilities, it is Parker's own example that authorizes Marvell's tactics. His instinct for parody is constantly gratified by Parker's writing: 'I must ask his pardon if I treat him too homely. It is his own fault that misled me' [p.7]. He picks up Parker's own confession of 'wild and rambling talk' and adds parenthetically '(as some will be forward enough to call it)' [pp.73–4]. Since the Anglican was among those dedicated to purging pulpit oratory of some of its excesses, Marvell notes more gleefully how his prose is 'bedawb'd with Rhetorick, and embroder'd so thick that you cannot discern the Ground' [p.12]. He doesn't allow *his* ground or argument to get obscured, but he responds in kind to Parker's style:

But therefore it was that I have before so particularly quoted and bound him up with his own Words as fast as such a Proteus could be pinion'd. For he is as waxen as the first matter, and no Form comes amiss to him.   [p.92]

His quotations let Parker condemn himself—'one may often gather more of his mind out of a word that drops casually, than out of his whole watchful and serious discourse' [p.67]. So much for a writer's considered prose! Or he sets passages from different sections side by side to reveal a work's inherent contradictions. His technique of moral criticism is, as Bradbrook and Thomas pointed out[84], 'often a literary criticism'. Anglican clergy, he notes, 'shew they are Pluralists [by never writing] in a modester stile than *We*' [p.106]. Parker's incapacity to argue and his confusion of terminology mark his deeper confusions over toleration and civil power. From using his opponent's language as symptom, Marvell proceeds with an ironic logic that Swift was also to employ more systematically to assume that Parker is only concerned with words and not what they refer to:

You find nothing but *Orthodoxy, Systems*, and *Syntagms, Polemical Theology, Subtilties* and *Distinctions. Demosthenes; Tankard-bearers; Pragmatical; Controversial:* General terms without foundation or reason assigned. That they seem like words of Cabal, & have no significance till they be decipher'd. Or, you would think he were playing at *Substantives* and *Adjectives*. All that rationally can be gathered from what he saith, is, that the Man is mad. [pp.32–3]

It is a variation of the perspectival games he'd played in 'Last Instructions', whereby great and small, heroic and pathetic, were interchanged. In *The Rehearsal Transpros'd* he also explores the implications of his perception that 'things are little or great according to the Eyes or Understanding of several men' [p.53].

For Marvell toleration of alternative ideas and beliefs to his own *was* a great matter, which Parker's understanding could not be allowed to diminish[85]. In the autumn of 1672, when he determined to publish *The Rehearsal Transpros'd*, it was crucial that 'men therefore are to be dealt with reasonably: and conscientious men by Conscience' [p.111]. Charles II seemed to concur, at least to judge by the Declaration of Indulgence, so Marvell found himself in the happy position of giving his support to the King for a measure which was everywhere else, even by Nonconformists who were suspicious of the tolerance extended to Roman Catholics, rejected. But Charles evidently liked Marvell's book for its own sake. Not exactly famous for literary taste—Marvell confidently tells Parker that the King 'never gave your Book the reading' [p.110]—Charles actually enjoyed *The Rehearsal Transpros'd*. One suspects that he liked, not just its thesis, but its colloquial conduct of the debate and perhaps passages like the following that glanced at himself amicably, if inaccurately (for Charles *did* wear 'Sacerdotal' dress at his Coronation):

But one thing I must confess is very pleasant, and he hath past an high Complement upon his Majesty in it: that he may, if he please, reserve the Priesthood and the Exercise of it to himself. Now this indeed is surprising; but this onely troubles me, how his Majesty would look in all the Sacerdotal habiliments,

62   *Charles II*, miniature
by Samuel Cooper, 1665.

and the Pontifical Wardrobe. I am afraid the King would find himself
incommoded with all that furniture upon his back, and would scarce reconcile
himself to wear even the Lawn-sleeves and the Surplice... But one thing I doubt
Mr *Bayes* did not well consider: that, if the King may discharge the Function of the
Priesthood, he may too (and 'tis all the reason in the world) assume the Revenue.

[p.51]

As a consequence Charles II (plate 62) liked the book enough to protect its
anonymous author from the authorities [*RT*.xxii]. Marvell bravely issued
the second part of the work with his own name on the title-page, on which
he also printed the concluding words of a threatening letter addressed to
him—'If thou darest to Print or Publish any Lie or Libel against Doctor
Parker, By the Eternal God I will cut thy Throat'. Such incidents did
occur, for in January 1671 Marvell had written to William Popple about
the attack on another Member, Sir John Coventry, who had 'almost all the
End of his Nose' cut off [II.321]. Marvell himself faced such dangers with

apparent equanimity, telling Parker how little he cares 'your threatning me here and in several other places with the loss of mine Ears, which however are yet in good plight, and apprehend no other danger, Mr. *Bayes* but to be of your Auditory' [p.202].

But the intolerance of both Anglican divines like Parker and, ironically, of the suspicious Nonconformists they attacked, worked to defeat the Declaration of Indulgence. Parliament first decided in 1673 that only it was enabled to suspend penal legislation and then went on to pass the Test Act against Roman Catholics. Marvell must again have been in a dilemma, continuing to believe in (at least) the inexpediency of persecution, but also distrusting Roman Catholicism, which meant the French alliance, French subsidies for the King to make him independent of Parliament, and the possible succession of the Roman Catholic Duke of York. His short-term solution to this dilemma was the second part of *The Rehearsal Transpros'd*, in which he answered various ripostes to the first, including one by Parker himself[86], and continued to shape his ideas of proper government. But in the long term what came to dominate his last five years was increasing exasperation with the King's inability and refusal to contribute his share to such a government; Parliament, too, bore its share of Marvell's disapproval, but it was essentially Charles's French policies and the resultant damage to his relations with Parliament that outraged Marvell.

The exact timetable and pattern of his allegiances is a matter of some dispute. Legouis talks of Marvell's 'third major political conversion' from support to (even seditious) rejection of the King (the earlier two, in his view, being from Charles I to Cromwell, and from Commonwealth to Restoration); Wallace, on the other hand, offers an intricate examination of Marvell's ultimate consistency, maintaining his faith in 'expedient government' but not 'expedient principles'[87]. It would be easy to take a leaf out of Marvell's book and argue that both are in part acceptable explanations. But a shift in his attitude to the King did occur ('conversion' being entirely too dramatic a notion to entertain of Marvell's subtle mind) *and* it was based upon his by now longstanding dedication as an M.P. to ensuring both a proper role in government for Parliament and a just representation of the nation's needs in that Parliament. This Marvell had the opportunity to make abundantly clear in the second part of *The Rehearsal Transpros'd*, issued during the winter of 1673-4.

It is in some respects a more serious and forthright document, where it addresses itself to matters of government, and a more scurrilous or personal one, when it answers the *ad hominem* attacks of those who had replied to the first part. He had been coarsely libelled by some of these antagonists and he generally responded in kind: Parker, for instance, was accused of allowing one of his curates to get his maidservant with child and then abort the pregnancy [p.212]. But Marvell also took the opportunity to set out some of the details of his own career, including his first meetings with Parker at Milton's home, and to defend most handsomely the latter's conduct (see above, pp.139–42).

But much of Marvell's energies and determination went into using the occasion of an enforced continuation of his quarrel with Parker to 'intermeddle', as he told Sir Edward Harley privately, 'in a noble and high argument' [II.328]. I suspect, too, that he also wished to make his way clear ahead, laying down the basic principles beyond which he would not move in the coming years. At the expense of some longer quotations, it is worth trying to see what he determined.

The Declaration of Indulgence having been withdrawn, Marvell was under no obligation to defend it, and he extended his argument against Parker's authoritarianism in matters of religion to include his anxieties about all 'Universal and Absolute Power' whether in civil or ecclesiastical matters [p.214]. The King's Declaration had been, from the parliamentary perspective, an unacceptable intrusion of royal power upon Parliament's prerogatives. Yet, equally, the intolerance of Anglican bishops had necessitated some remedy from the King himself. So Marvell is forced to 'explain my self as distinctly as I can, and as close as possible what is mine own opinion in this matter of the Magistrate and Government' [p.232].

What guides his deliberations is, characteristically, a recognition both of essential principles and of expediency. 'The Power of the Magistrate', he affirms from the start, 'does most certainly issue from the Divine Authority. The Obedience due to that Power is by Divine Command; and Subjects are bound both as Men and as Christians to obey the Magistrate Actively in all things where their Duty to God intercedes not' [pp.232–3]. However, the 'modester Question' to pose the Magistrate is 'how far it is advisable. . .to exert and push the rigour of that Power which no man can deny him' [ibid.]. Thus does Marvell establish a common-sensical basis for the succeeding pages. It is an attitude that also informs his pragmatic assessment of inevitable sicknesses in the body politic:

For all Governments and Societies of men, and so the Ecclesiastical, do in process of long time gather an irregularity, and wear away much of their primitive institution. And therefore the true wisdom of all Ages hath been to review at fit periods those errours, defects or excesses, that have insensibly crept on into the Publick Administration; to brush the dust off the Wheels, and oyl them again, or if it be found advisable to chuse a set of new ones.   [p.239]

This flexibility and self-adaptation to new times and conditions comes aptly from Marvell, whose own political allegiances had adjusted themselves to various regimes since the 1640s. This 'Reformation', he continues, 'is most easily and with least disturbance to be effected by the Society it self, no single men being forbidden by any Magistrate to amend their own manners, and much more all Societies having the liberty to bring themselves within compass'. It is the role of the Magistrate to renew and preserve 'publick wellfare' when 'men themselves shall omit their duty in this matter'. His obligation is the greater because the only alternative is action by the people themselves, 'from which God defend every good Government' [p.240]:

For though all Commotions be unlawful, yet by this means they prove unavoidable. In all times that are insensible there is nevertheless a natural force alwayes operating to expel and reject whatsoever is contrary to their subsistence. And the sensible but brutish creatures heard together as if it were in counsel against their common inconveniences, and imbolden'd by their multitude, rebel even against Man their Lord and Master. And the Common People in all places partake so much of Sense and Nature, that, could they be imagined and contrived to be irrational, yet they would ferment and tumultuate at last for their own preservation. Yet neither do they want the use of Reason, and perhaps their aggregated Judgement discerns most truly the errours of Government, forasmuch as they are the first to be sure that smart under them. In this only they come to be short-sighted, that though they know the Diseases, they understood not the Remedies, and though good Patients, they are ill Physicians.   [p.240]

But if the Magistrate only can initiate 'a just and effectual Reformation...especialy among the Ecclesiasticks' [p.240], the cause *must* be a good one, so that his power is not wasted 'in a matter so unnecessary, so trivial, and so pernicious to the publick Quiet' as Parker had originally proposed [p.242]. And the Magistrate's own awareness of his divine sanction in a 'Providential constitution' [p.250] will recall him to a fundamental (and always vulnerable) humanity: 'his Administration is humane [i.e. human], neither is it possible either for him to exact or men to pay him more then a Civil obedience in those Laws which he constituteth' [p.250].

These wise, but also perhaps naive, expectations of Restoration government were never realized. Marvell found that he could not count upon the King's 'universal Benignity towards [his] Subjects' [p.233]. Nor could he rely—his Coy Mistress, if still alive, could have reminded him of this—upon the concurrence of time to accomplish 'a great and durable design' [p.234]. Toleration did not prosper, and the King's relationship with Parliament drastically worsened. Indeed, Parliament was simply not allowed to meet—being in session for only eight months between April 1671 and December 1676 and again for only the first half of the next year. In 1677 Marvell protested against being 'kickt from adjournment to adjournment, as from one stair down to another, and when they were at the bottom kickt up again, having no mind yet to go *out of doors*' [Grosart, IV.410]. And when the House did sit, it was dismaying to witness its divisiveness and corruption, its similarity to the playhouse ('all Sorts of People flocking thither, and paying their Mony as at a common

Playhouse', II.342). Marvell could voice his dismay in private letters to William Popple. In 1675 he also took the more dangerous step of writing and (presumably) allowing to circulate in manuscript a 'Mock Speech from the Throne'[88].

In a letter to Hull of 13 April Marvell gave the 'official' version of the King's speech which he'd heard that day. Charles had promised 'security of...Religion and Property' and 'to establish a durable Correspondence betwixt him and his People'; but he also reminded them that 'the Navy did stand in need of repairing and increasing'. Marvell apologizes to the Mayor for 'this summary relation', promising to send the speech when it was printed. Perhaps he was, in fact, already spending his time in drafting the parody, which captures so keenly both a speaking tone and the King's essential interests:

Some of you may perhaps think it dangerous to make me too rich, but doe not fear it, for I promise you faithfully, whatsoever You will give I will always take care to want; for the truth of which you may rely upon the word of a King.
. . .
Here is my Ld Treas^r can tell you that all the Mony designed for the Summer Guards must of necessity be employ'd to the next Yeares Cradles and Swadling-Cloths [for his bastard offspring]. What then shall we do for ships?
. . .
The Nation hates you already, for giving so much, and I will hate you now if you doe not give me more. So that now your Interest obliges You to stick to me or you will not have a friend left in England. On the other side, if you will continue the Revenue as desired, I shall be inabled to performe those Great things for Your Religion and Libertye which I have had long in my Thoughts, but cannot effect them without this Establishment. Therefore look to it, if You do not make me Rich enough to undoe You, it shall lye at your dores.

As an example of the King's 'Zeal' Marvell makes him tell of 'converting all my Natural Sons from Popery...It would do Your Heart good to hear how prettily little George can read in the Psalter'. It was, of course, the legitimate heir to the throne, James, Duke of York, who was the Roman Catholic! The parody also makes much irony out of the House's current petition for the removal of the Duke of Lauderdale and its attempt to impeach the Lord Treasurer, Danby, both of whom Charles is made to praise extravagantly, stressing the 'Credit' they have with his listeners (presumably in more senses than one).

Marvell was also engaged in some verse satires at the King's expense, though, as with the 'Mock Speech', the attributions are not absolutely reliable (for the details see the notes in I.376 ff). Sometime in 1674 he had jauntily celebrated Sir Robert Viner's erection of a statue of Charles II at Woolchurch Market (where the Mansion House is now). The statue, still preserved at Newby Hall in Yorkshire (plate 63), was cobbled up out

63 Equestrian statue of Charles II trampling Oliver Cromwell, erected in London in 1675.

of one representing John Sobieski, King of Poland, trampling a Turk, and converted by the loyal merchant into Charles trampling Cromwell. Marvell finds everything about it aptly expressive:

> But a market, they say, does suit the king well,
> Who the Parliament buys and revenues does sell,
> And others to make the similitude hold
> Say his Majesty himself is bought too and sold.   [p.188]

177

(The last line being probably a reference to the secret Treaty of Dover, where Charles 'sold' himself to Louis.) In another set of doggerel verses, parodying the songs performed on such occasions, Marvell describes the same Viner, now Lord Mayor of London, bestowing the city's freedom upon the King [pp.190–4]. Charles's lifestyle can readily—the ease is part of the joke—be adapted to that of the typical apprentice:

> He ne're knew not he
> How to serve or be free,
> Tho he has past through so many Adventures;
> But e're since he was bound
> ('Tis the same to be Crown'd)
> Has every Day broke his Indentures.
>
> He spends all his Days
> In runing to Plays,
> When in his Shop he shou'd be poreing;
> And wasts all his Nights
> In his constant Delights
> Of Revelling, Drinking and Whoreing.

The range of complaint, as other poems reveal, is from debauchery ('Lew'd Court in drunken slumbers', p.194) through venal corruption ('A Colony of French Possess the Court', p.195) to incompetence ('this is a heavier Curse/That suck and draine thus ev'ry Purse/By this old Whitehall Pump', p.208). The anger and frustration, if they are Marvell's work, are barely contained by the humour generated in the satires. The impossibility for the former Cavalier lover ('Till the Conversion of the Jews') becomes the despair of the present member of the Cavalier Parliament ('Till Charles loves Parliaments, till James hates Rome', p.194). The whole catalogue of grievances is rehearsed in 'A Dialogue between the Two Horses' [pp.208–213] at the Woolchurch Market and at Charing Cross, the latter being a statue of Charles I re-erected by Danby in 1675. The piece, however, goes somewhat further in expressing its abhorrence of political life in the 1670s. Even allowing for the grotesque exaggeration of popular lampoons, it is still rather startling to think that Marvell (though his authorship *is* especially doubtful here) could have become so far alienated as to make the Woolchurch horse—that is, Charles II's (with Cromwell underneath it)—

> freely declare it, I am for old Noll.
> Tho' his Government did a Tyrants resemble,
> Hee made England great and it's enemies tremble
> . . .
> Ch But canst thou Divine when things shall be mended?
> W   When the Reign of the Line of the Stuarts is ended.

...
A Commonwealth a Common-wealth wee proclaim to
    the Nacion;
The Gods have repented the Kings Restoration.

The horses, in mid-dialogue, pause to consider the danger of their candour ('Yet truth many times being punish't for Treason'). A year earlier Marvell—and here there is at any rate no doubt of his authorship—contributed a poem to the second edition of his friend's *Paradise Lost* [pp.137–9]. This fine tribute to Milton celebrates larger and more fearsome truths than Marvell, for all his recklessness, was able to make the subject of his song at that time. His own verse satires employ 'tinkling Rhime', which Milton's epic 'needs not'. Read now, as they were written then, in the midst of Marvell's depressing and frustrating political career, the lines take on a fresh significance. Underlying them is surely an acknowledgement of Milton's own abandonment of an active political life for

> *Messiah* Crown'd, *Gods* Reconcil'd Decree,
> Rebelling *Angels*, the Forbidden Tree,
> Heav'n, Hell, Earth, Chaos, All.

The trivial times may even 'presume the whole Creations day/To change in Scenes, and show it in a Play'. That alludes to Dryden's 'Heroick Opera', published as *The State of Innocence, and Fall of Man*. The reference elevates *Paradise Lost* above a world where everything from the Dutch in the Medway to a session of the House of Commons *and* Man's Fall would be trivialized into yet another theatrical entertainment for the Court gallants. The opening conceit, where Marvell fears 'That he would ruine (for I saw him strong)/The sacred Truths to Fable and old Song', is transformed into humble acknowledgement that sacred truths may survive and flourish in 'slender Book':

> That Majesty which through thy Work doth Reign
> Draws the Devout, deterring the Profane.
> And things divine thou treatst of in such state
> As them preserves, and Thee inviolate.
> At once delight and horrour on us seize,
> Thou singst with so much gravity and ease;
> And above humane flight dost soar aloft,
> With Plume so strong, so equal, and so soft.
> The *Bird* nam'd from that *Paradise* you sing
> So never Flags, but alwaies keeps on Wing.

Whether or not it is fully realized, and whether a question of regret, pride or objective recognition of the contrast, the difference between them is strong: the blind poet, prophetic of a 'Paradise within thee, happier far'; the younger and sighted commentator upon contemporary events, needing to 'sequester my self one whole Day at Highgate' from the 'Busyness of Parliament last sitting' [II.341].

Enforced leisure from the frequently prorogued sessions was employed by Marvell in composing further pamphlets. In 1676 he continued his attacks on the Anglican hierarchy and urged toleration for dissenters in *Mr Smirke: Or, The Divine in Mode*. Its occasion was an exchange of anonymous pamphlets, *The Naked Truth* by the Bishop of Hereford, Herbert Croft, answered by some rude *Animadversions* from Francis Turner, Master of St John's College, Cambridge, and Chaplain to the Duke of York. Again, Marvell takes his title from a minor character in Etherege's play, *The Man of Mode*, and makes of his opponent a similar butt to those we find among the 'false wits' of Restoration comedy: 'he took up an unfortunate resolution that he would be witty: infortunate, I say, and no less criminal; for I dare aver that never any person was more manifestly guilty of the sin against nature' [Grosart, IV.11]. His method, as with Parker four years before, was to start through the 'whole pedler's-pack of [Turner's] malice'; but he finds the pages full of insolence and absurdity, remarking that 'calumny is like London dirt, with which though a man may be spattered in an instant, yet it requires much time, pains, and fullers-earth to scoure it out again' [ibid.p.28]. He pretends to (or really does) get bored ('I am weary of such stuffe, both mine own and his') and instead appends 'A Short Historical Essay touching General Councils, Creeds, and Imposition in Religion'. Still directed against the authority of bishops—though attached to a defence of one—the 'Essay' (as to some extent the first part of *Mr Smirke*) marks a sudden change in Marvell's conduct of controversy. Gone are the twisting, teasing and unpredictable sentences; instead, the prose moves ahead smoothly, with more decorum and more (though not exceptional) attention to the logic of argument:

So that having cast about, in this summary again, (whereby it plainly appears, that according to natural right and the apprehension of all sober heathen governours, Christianity, as a religion, was wholly exempt from the Magistrates jurisdiction or lawes, farther than any particular person among them immorally transgress'd, as others, the common rules of human society) I cannot but return to the question with which I begun. What was the matter? How came it about that Christianity, which approv'd itself under all persecutions to the heathen emperours, and merited their favour so far, till at last it regularly succeeded to the monarchy, should, under those of their own profession, be more distressed? But the answer is now much shorter and certainer: and I will adventure boldly to say, the true and single cause then was the bishops. [ibid. pp.151–2]

In July he told Sir Edward Harley that 'the book said to be Marvels makes what shift it can in the world but the Author walks negligently up and down as unconcerned. The Divines of our Church say it is not in the merry part as good as the Rehearsall Transpros'd' [II.346]. He continued to denounce bishops in a Latin poem on James Mitchell, tortured and executed in Scotland for the attempted murder of Archbishop Sharp, who is urged, though he scorns God, to respect his fellow humans [I.213–14].

A tired and corrupt Parliament started its fifteenth session in mid-February 1677. There were immediate attempts to secure a dissolution and hold new elections. Although the Commons proceeded rather gingerly, the Lords debated it with so much 'more earnessnesse' [II.178] that Danby arranged that four of them, including Marvell's correspondent Wharton, Shaftesbury and Buckingham, were sent to the Tower [II.179]. 'Thus a prorogation without precedent', wrote Marvell, 'was to be warranted by an imprisonment without example' [Grosart, IV.322]. Danby's next manoeuvres were designed to strengthen the powers of the bishops, including 'An Act for further securing the Protestant Religion, by educating the Children of the Royal Family therein'. Although Marvell must have appreciated the move against Roman Catholicism, he could hardly have accepted a further enhancement of the bishops' intolerable authority; he attacked it in the House on 27 March 1677 in a long speech, for which he apologized by saying he was unaccustomed to speaking, but forcibly declared that 'whether this Bill will prevent Popery or not, this will secure the provisions of the Bishops' [Grosart, II.xxxi]. When a couple of days later Marvell was involved in a friendly scuffle with Sir Philip Harcourt in the chamber, the Speaker tried to get his own back by drawing the House's attention to it; Marvell's quick temper led him to retort that the Speaker should 'keep himself in Order', and it was only his equally quick-witted retreat to a humble apology that probably prevented his dispatch to the Tower[89].

The Commons (and in this matter, somewhat confusingly, Danby) wanted a war against France in alliance with the Protestant Prince of Orange, recently married to Mary, daughter of the Duke of York. But they refused to vote the subsidies until they received a clear account from the King of how he intended to use it. The stalemate ('there will be no mony given this sitting but upon very visible and effectuall termes', II.201) resulted in two further adjournments in May and July. Marvell was provoked now into beginning another pamphlet, *An Account of the Growth of Popery and Arbitrary Government in England,* which he continued writing during the autumn and winter of 1677. This time he was not drawn into controversy by others' work, but wrote on his own account, and, I suspect, out of sheer frustration with parliamentary deadlock and inefficiency, chose once again to see what he could do anonymously outside the House.

The title indicates the double strain of his argument. He provides an intricate and detailed history of recent government, drawing extensively on official documents. He is also concerned to show that all naval humiliations, all the wretched impasse of Government business, were caused by the insidious workings of what he calls 'Papist conspirators' [Grosart, IV.262], notably the French King. He chooses not to attack Charles II, perhaps out of caution (though the rest of the work does not support that explanation); more likely out of confidence that he might still persuade all his advisors and collaborators of their senseless enterprise and thus bring the King to order without having to attack him in person. To indicate how late such a change of heart has been left, Marvell invokes once again the King's favourite imagery of the playhouse: 'It is now come to the fourth act, and the next scene that opens may be Rome or Paris, yet men sit by, like idle spectators, and still give money towards their own tragedy' [ibid. p.412].

Through the whole work speaks a convinced parliamentary man—not only in his detailed and inside knowledge of its workings or non-workings between 1675 and December 1677, but also in his implicit confidence in Parliament's necessary role in a proper government:

the subjects retain their proportion in the Legislature; the very meanest commoner of England is represented in Parliament, and is a party to those laws by which the Prince is sworn to govern himself and his people.   [ibid. pp.248–9]

Upon that premise, lengthily and passionately explained at the start, Marvell bases his earnest, intense plea for what, in the final paragraph, he calls a deliverance from 'all privy conspiracy...all iniquity and ...flatterers'. Throughout he relies upon the clear prose style, first tried in the 'Essay on Councils', and here deployed as the voice for 'the same incorrupt mind and cleare Conscience' of which he boasted to his constituents [II.177]; but he uses it with a conviction and courage that in the same correspondence he thought less prudent—'But they that discourse the lest and thinke the best... will be the wisest men and the best Subjects' [II.234]. Frankness on his part authorizes his plea for honesty and openness throughout the nation:

All that they desired was, that his Majesty and his people unanimously, truly, sincerely and thoroughly declare and engage in this business, with a mutual confidence speaking out on both sides, and this, and nothing but this, would discharge and extinguish all jealousies.   [Grosart, IV.366]

Yet he was not a Hull man for nothing, and the *Growth of Popery* makes much (quite accurately) of French maritime aggression in the Channel and ends with an appendix on English shipping lost to French privateers since 1673.

The Growth of Popery caused a stir in Government circles in 1678; its printer was imprisoned, and a reward offered for identifying its author. On 10 June Marvell wrote impishly to his nephew that 'Three or four printed Books since have described, as near as it was proper to go, the Man being a Member of Parliament, Mr *Marvell* to have been the Author; but if he had, surely he should not have escaped being questioned in Parliament, or some other Place' [II.357]. As an expression of opposition ideology Marvell's book was to be widely influential: in the long term upon the nascent Whig party, more immediately upon the events of the Popish Plot in the autumn of 1678 and the succeeding Exclusion Crisis. As M.P. for Kingston upon Hull Marvell had many cordial meetings with the town's High Steward, the Duke of Monmouth [see II.206–7]. Whether he would have supported Shaftesbury's armed promotion of Monmouth as Protestant successor to Charles II, and what he would have thought of Titus Oates, we may surmise, but cannot know. For by then Andrew Marvell was dead.

10 Scarse fully paralleled by any

He died on 16 August 1678 at a house he had rented the previous year in Great Russell Street. He had just returned from a rare visit to Hull and must have caught a fever on the journey down. It was rumoured that he had been poisoned by Jesuits, but, as we now know[90], the irony is that he was bled and sweated by an old-fashioned doctor who stubbornly refused to administer a dose of 'Jesuits' powder' or *cortex peruvianus* which might have cured his ague. He was buried in St Giles-in-the-Fields on 18 August, the Hull Corporation meeting the expenses of the funeral and of a memorial tablet.

In 1681 were published his *Miscellaneous Poems,* the title page of which (plate 64) declared their author to have been a 'Late Member of the Honourable House of Commons'. This volume must have caused his friends, as it causes his later biographers and critics, something of a shock; for a notice 'To The Reader' declared—

These are to Certifie every Ingenious Reader, that all these Poems, as also the

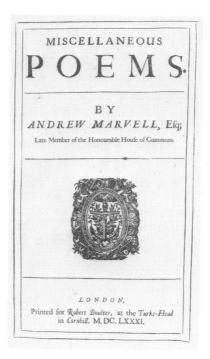

MISCELLANEOUS
POEMS.

BY
ANDREW MARVELL, Efq;
Late Member of the Honourable Houfe of Commons.

LONDON,
Printed for *Robert Boulter,* at the *Turks-Head*
in *Cornhill.* M. DC. LXXXI.

64   Title page of *Miscellaneous Poems,* 1681.

other things in this Book contained, are Printed according to the exact Copies of
my late dear Husband, under his own Hand-Writing, being found since his Death
among his other Papers, Witness my Hand this 15 *th* day of *October,* 1680.

Mary Marvell.

'Mrs Marvell', alias Mrs Palmer, widow of a poor keeper of a tennis court
and mother of several children, has only recently emerged into something·
like clarity from a quite astonishing tangle of litigation and human
machinations. She was Marvell's landlady when he had lodgings in
Westminster, and the year before he died he had taken the Great Russell
Street house in her name. In this house he concealed some friends, distant
connections from Hull, who were bankrupts and in flight from the law
and their creditors. A sum of five hundred pounds belonging to one of
them, Edward Nelthorpe, was deposited in Marvell's name with a
goldsmith. After the poet's death, to prevent the money accruing to his
estate, they had recourse to various stratagems, in which Mary Palmer and
another bankrupt, John Farrington, then in prison, all joined. It was
during these dealings and eight months after Marvell's death that she
assumed his name for the legal purpose of claiming the money for her
partners and preventing it being seized by the Bankruptcy

Commissioners. It was probably only when she needed some kind of evidence to substantiate her story of being Marvell's widow that she published the *Miscellaneous Poems* from among 'a few Books and papers of a small value' which she said she had found in Marvell's Maiden Lane lodgings in Covent Garden after the rest of his effects had been taken by Farrington. During a falling out among the conspirators she actually defended her claim by naming the time and place of the 'marriage'—May 1667 at Holy Trinity in the Little Minories. Yet the registers for that period are lost, even presumed by Tupper to have been stolen, though it all sounds too melodramatic. To confuse matters further, she was buried under her own name. Her fellow schemer's claim that she was not Mrs Marvell—'nor is it probable that the said Andrew Marvell who was a Member of the house of Comons for many year together & a very learned man would undervalue himselfe to intermarry with so mean a pson as shee the said Mary'—was precisely the reason she, in her turn, gave for keeping it secret. It is also, we might think, a reason to appeal to Marvell's delight in contrary states and to his strangely guarded privacy. On the other hand, it all sounds like the angry squabbling of litigants, and on the face of it the evidence is strongly against her marriage to Marvell: she waited rather long after his death to claim her kinship; she couldn't remember the day of his death; she ceased to use his name once the bankrupts had obtained their money in 1684. 'Mrs Marvell', in short, would clearly seem to be, in a phrase the poet himself would have appreciated, a 'legal fiction', were it not (to swing the argument back once again) that the Prerogative Court of Canterbury did allow her claim.

Yet it is typical of the shadows that surround so much of Marvell's life that, despite the profusion of documents in this instance, so many questions still remain unanswered. Why, for example, was he sheltering Nelthorpe and Richard Thompson in the first place? Was it compassion for those on the run, friendship or family ties, pecuniary obligations (Farrington testified that Marvell was practically penniless during his last years), business interests (maybe Marvell's Russian experience had been put at the service of their 'several advantagious or profitable Trades. . . to *Russia*'), or political sympathies (both Nelthorpe and Thompson were anti-Royalist and trouble-makers in the Common Council)? But these final mysteries, of course, are merely the end of a longer list of enigmas and lacunae that confront Marvell's biographer. One needs to know more about *when* he wrote individual poems, *whether* he is indeed the author of the Restoration satires assigned or not assigned to him, what *in fact* (rather than in my suppositions) he did see during those four years abroad, what at various stages of his career were his political affiliations—why, for instance, when his suspicions of the French seem to have been aroused in 1670, did he compose 'Inscribenda Luparae' [I.56–7], laudatory distichs on Louis XIV's newly completed Louvre? An especially urgent need is to find out more about his involvement in 1659 with James Harrington's Rota Club which met at Miles Coffee House and debated ideal forms of government.

Linked to the mysteries are the myths. Around the final, political and parliamentary, phase of his career grew up legends which elaborated the image of an incorruptible antagonist to the Court interests. The memorial, for which Hull Corporation apparently paid, was reportedly refused by the rector of St Giles-in-the-Fields or, in another legend, demolished by Royalist zealots in 1682[91]. There is also the story of the attempt by Danby, the Lord Treasurer, to bribe Marvell: it recounts how the King sent Danby to climb up 'two Pair of Stairs' to the poet's lodgings near the Strand and tell 'him that he came with a Message from his Majesty, which was to know what he could do to serve him'; Marvell answered 'in his usual facetious way'. That version is at least consonant with Marvell's own scorn for M.P.s who 'are all of them to be bought and sold' [Grosart, IV.328]. A later version elaborates an edifying exchange between the poet and his servant in front of the Lord Treasurer: 'Jack, child, what had I for dinner yesterday?' 'Don't you remember, sir? You had the little shoulder of mutton that you ordered me to bring from a woman in the market.' 'Very right, child. What have I for dinner today?' 'Don't you know, sir, that you bid me lay by the blade-bone to broil?' ''Tis so, very right, child, go away'[92].

Yet there are also hints that connect Marvell with 'undercover' activities. An enigmatic entry in the *Calendar of State Papers* for 1671 links his name with Buckingham's and that of Colonel Thomas Blood in some anti-French espionage (there *is* a connection between Blood and the poet, who wrote a Latin epigram [I.178] on the former's attempt, while disguised as a parson, to steal the Crown Jewels). Later there are hints of Marvell's being a spy for the Prince of Orange and working as part of a Dutch fifth column in England[93]. Marvell himself provides a wry commentary upon all these hints and rumours in a private letter to Sir Edward Harley: 'some years agoe I heard that he [a Dr Bates] said Marvell was an Intelligencer to the King of France. Twas about the same time that the Doctor was in pension to another Monarch. I know not what to say . . .' [II.346].

It was Marvell's political rather than his poetical career that was cherished for a long time after his death. As late as the nineteenth century a statue erected in his native Hull and still preserved outside the new Grammar School (plate 65) totally neglected to mention that he had been a poet. As 'patriot', as 'this Islands watchful Centinel'[94], is how his reputation was preserved, with the odd exception of something like Swift's literary 'pleasure' at reading *The Rehearsal Transpros'd* or the inclusion of nine lyrics in the 1727 *Tonson's Miscellany*. In 1821 Lamb quoted some stanzas of 'The Garden' in his *Essays of Elia*; but, despite

65 Statue of Andrew Marvell, erected in Hull, nineteenth century.

Legouis' incredulity, the 'garden-loving' poet, as Lamb termed him, barely touched the Romantic imagination. Wordsworth noted him as a satirist and celebrated his friendship with Milton. The change was perhaps initiated in 1861 when Palgrave included three selections in *The Golden Treasury*.

Modern literary and critical taste has more than made up for the earlier neglect of Marvell's poetry, even though it cannot entirely absorb all the political verses. A biographer's perspective will inevitably be different. While the critic will express dismay (rightly) that an imagination that produced the 'Horatian Ode' also contrived 'Tom May's Death' soon afterwards, a biographer will want to insist, in even that most problematical case, upon the repercussions of a man's contrariness. Marvell's instinct to look at life's variousness is something that his best poetry everywhere declares. Its language encourages and accommodates ambiguity; dialogue, like controversy later, is its explicit or implicit form; a characteristic stance is its propensity to explore alternatives or even, in conceit, to make the most of unsatisfactory conditions, as when the eunuch poet is reassured that 'Fame shall be ever pregnant by thy verse' [I.57]. And 'The Garden' praises a natural and uncomplicated existence only to discover that, first, it is too perfect a paradise and, second, that it was contrived by the 'skilful Gardner' anyway. 'Equally', as John Wallace reminds us, is one of his favourite words, just as antithesis is apparently the most used figure in his Latin poetry[95].

Both 'The Garden' and 'Upon Appleton House' recognize that gardens are where heroic activism is sidetracked or abandoned as well as recuperated. But while Marvell could have learnt that from Spenser, Tasso, Ariosto or Milton, it was, I suspect, also one of his own deeply held convictions. The image of armour rusting on a hook in the hall occurs in both the 'Horatian Ode' and *The Rehearsal Transpros'd* and in both it inaugurates fresh activity: yet, typically, in the former he eventually praises the energy, while in the latter it is mocked [p.120]. Marvell often voices his instinct for retired contemplation; it was a commonplace of the time, to which his fine version of some lines from Seneca contributes:

> Climb at *Court* for me that will
> Tottering favors Pinacle;
> All I seek is to lye still.
> Settled in some secret Nest
> In calm Leisure let me rest;
> And far of the publick Stage
> Pass away my silent Age.
> Thus when without noise, unknown,
> I have liv'd out all my span,
> I shall dye, without a groan,
> An old honest Country man.

> Who exposed to others Ey's,
> Into his own Heart ne'r pry's,
> Death to him's a Strange surprise   [p.58]

At the end of his life he confessed to a Mayor of Hull that 'I am naturally and now more by my Age inclined to keep my thoughts private' [II.166]. Yet it is an inclination that he frequently forgoes; or did he voice it often because he knew he could never keep the resolution, 'not to write at all is much the safer course of life'? Still, he continues with—

> but if a mans Fate or *Genius* prompt him otherwise, 'tis necessary that he be copious in matter, solid in reason, methodical in the order of his work; and that the subject be well chosen, the season well fix'd, and, to be short, that his whole production be matur'd to see the light by a just course of time, and judicious deliberation.   [*RT*.159–60]

His deliberate surrender of himself to the exigencies of time and place was, by his own criteria expressed there, his genius. He urged such a philosophy upon his coy mistress and upon Archdeacon Parker—'all laws however are but Probationers of Time' [*RT*.251]. He responded with ease to various situations, delighting in different voices, different disguises, different genres. As a Cavalier lyricist, at Eton or at Westminster he absorbed local colour to the point almost of mimicry, yet without abandoning his own integrity. It is a rare occurrence when we cannot hear his voice through the lampoonist's style as in, say, 'A Ballad call'd the Chequer Inn' [pp.201–8], though it is not clear that Marvell is the author. It may well be that we can explain the difference between his Restoration writing and his lyrics by invoking the creative leisure, 'the *otia sana* of Nun-Appleton and Eton, and the lack of it in Restoration London'[96]. But we must also acknowledge his readiness to respond to every context in which he found himself.

A continuing coherence of idea and personality beneath the disguises is clear in many ways—nor is it just the consistent adoption of them. It is there in his concern for those subjected to the forces of intolerance—his last letters speak of his sympathy for the persecuted Scottish Covenanters (see II.357), and his last pamphlet was in defence of John Howe, a former chaplain of Cromwell's [Grosart, IV.162–242]. He was loyal, brave and outspoken, tough to the point of verbal or physical violence, when they were necessary. But this did not warrant, for example, either denying his instinct for examining rival ideas ('Tom May', again), or neglecting the proprieties of his role of M.P. (in letters to Hull) or of diplomatic secretary (denouncing the regicides in official speeches to the Czar).

But above all there is his continuing devotion to poetry. Critics talk of his lyrics and his Restoration poetry as separate and unrelated compartments of his life. But his editors give occasional grounds for suspecting that those 'papers of a small value' which Mary Palmer came upon and turned into *Miscellaneous Poems* were the fruit of self-critical, if intermittent, revision[97]. He was unlikely to miss the application to his manuscripts of one of his observations upon political and moral conduct: ''Tis pride that makes a Rebel,' he wrote, consoling Sir John Trott for the loss of his two sons, 'And nothing but the over-weening of our selves and our own things that raises us against divine Providence' [II.312]. Such a belief sustains both his apparent indifference to publication of his poems during his lifetime and, if the hints are right, his recurrent scrutiny and reworking of them. The poems that the printer of 1681, in a moment of panic or caution, decided to drop from *Miscellaneous Poems* were those which we guess must have mattered much to Marvell at the time of their first drafting and continued to matter: 'An Horatian Ode', 'The First Anniversary' and half of 'A Poem upon the Death of O.C.' were cancelled from all but the British Library copy. That these had to wait until 1776 to join the rest of the *oeuvre* was something that, provided they survived, which they luckily did, Marvell would presumably have accepted.

Though we do not have much evidence of Marvell's private and inward life, it is delivered most openly in the letters to his nephew. William Popple's epitaph on his uncle, then, is an appropriate conclusion. It is given a proper lapidary colouring and stiffness; yet the phrase taken as the title of this section—'scarse fully paralleled by any'—has a quite Marvellian relish of ambiguity. Popple's judgement, even if unintended, is ultimately and properly a literary one.

...joining the most peculiar Graces of Wit and Learning/With an singular Penetration and Strength of Judgement/And Exercising all these, in the whole Course of his Life/With an unalterable Steadiness in the Ways of Virtue/He became the Ornament and Example of his Age/Beloved by Good Men, feard by Bad, admired by All,/Though imitated alas by few, and scarse fully paralleled by any[98].

66 *Andrew Marvell*. minature by Samuel Cooper (?), see note on p.199.

Notes

All quotations from Marvell are taken, unless otherwise stated, from *The Poems and Letters of Andrew Marvell*, ed. H.M. Margoliouth, 3rd ed., revised by Pierre Legouis with the collaboration of E.E. Duncan-Jones (Oxford, 1971); references are given in square brackets to either vol. I (Poems) or II (Letters). Quotations from *The Rehearsal Transpros'd*, ed. D.I.B. Smith (Oxford, 1971) are indicated by the abbreviation *RT*. Quotations from both the above editions are by permission of Oxford University Press. All other references to Marvell's writings are from *The Complete Works in Verse and Prose of Andrew Marvell M.P.*, ed. Alexander B. Grosart, 4 vols. (priv. printed 1872), abbreviated as 'Grosart' with the relevant volume number. For Marvell's Latin poetry I have also relied upon *The Latin Poetry of Andrew Marvell*, ed. with commentaries by W.A. McQueen and K.A. Rockwell, University of N. Carolina Studies in Comparative literature 34 (Chapel Hill, 1964).

1. *The Works of Andrew Marvell*, 3 vols. (1776), III.489.
2. For this and all other quotations from Aubrey see the Penguin edition of *Brief Lives* (1972), pp.356–7; for Parker, see below, note 13; Milton's letter to Bradshaw of 21 February 1652/3 is in *The Life Records of John Milton*, ed. J. Milton French (Rutgers, New Jersey, 1949–58), III.322–3; Dryden's reference in the Preface to *Religio Laici* is in *Poems and Fables*, ed. James Kinsley (1970), p.279; Rochester's reference is in *The Complete Poems*, ed. D.M. Vieth (New Haven, 1968), p.76; for other references and details of further attacks see M.C. Bradbrook and M.G. Lloyd Thomas, *Andrew Marvell* (Cambridge, 1940), pp.12 and 18ff.
3. See *Catalogue of Seventeenth-Century Portraits in the National Portrait Gallery*, compiled by David Piper (Cambridge, 1963), pp.221–2. For the Hanneman portrait see also the *Bulletin* of Ferens Art Gallery, Hull (July–September 1963). For help with Marvell's portraits I am grateful to Mr Malcolm Rogers of the National Portrait Gallery and Mr John Ingamells of the Wallace Collection.
4. *Of the Characters of Women* (1735), later Moral Essay II, lines 7–14. On this passage and its fellow feeling with Montaigne see my *The Figure in the Landscape. Poetry, Painting and Gardening during the Eighteenth Century* (Baltimore, 1976), pp.90 and 257.
5. John M. Wallace, *Destiny His Choice, The Loyalism of Andrew Marvell* (Cambridge, 1968), pp.8, 228 and *passim*. This is the most sustained attempt to read Marvell's career in the light of contemporary politics, though sometimes the poetry gets rather submerged.
6. Edmund Hickeringill, *Gregory Father Greybeard* (1673), pp.35, 138, 172, 207 and *passim*.
7. See Thompson, ed. cit., I. lvii. The contrast is also made by Bradbrook and Thomas, op.cit., p.11.
8. Respectively, *Walpole Society Publications*, XX (Vertue Note Books II), pp.2 and 22, and J.L. Propert, *History of Miniature Art* (London and New York, 1887), p.246. A further portrait of 'Marvell' was illustrated in *The Connoisseur*, XV (1906), p.227, as Mrs Duncan-Jones has kindly pointed out to me. Redgrove's remark on putative portraits of famous men is quoted from Leo Miller, 'Milton's Portraits. An *Impartial* Inquiry into their Authentication', *Milton Quarterly*, special

issue (1976), which explores a parallel problem to the one of Marvell's iconography.

9.   L.N. Wall, 'Andrew Marvell of Meldreth', *Notes and Queries* (September 1958), pp.399–400, which is also the source of my references later in the same paragraph to the poet's grandfather. The house known as The Marvells is alluded to by Pierre Legouis (citing Grosart), *Andrew Marvell. Poet. Puritan. Patriot* (Oxford, 1965), p.1. This study by Legouis is a revised but shortened version in English of his earlier and detailed study, *André Marvell. Poète, puritain, patriote* (Paris and London, 1928), to which reference will also occasionally have to be made for documentation not included in the English version. My indebtedness to these studies will be apparent throughout.

10.   Anthony à Wood, *Athenae Oxonienses*, ed. Bliss (1813–20), IV.231.

11.   *A Reproof of the Rehearsal Transpros'd* (1673), pp.341–2. For the Fuller quotation see *The Worthies of England*, ed. John Freeman (1952), p.58. Legouis, *André Marvell*, pp.4–5 and 18–9, notes various animosities that also transpired between the lecturer and citizens of Hull.

12.   Wood, ed. cit., IV.232.

13.   Grosart, IV.15. On seventeenth-century education see, among others, M. Curtis, *Oxford and Cambridge in Transition* (1959) and John R. Mulder, *The Temple of the Mind. Education and Literary Taste in Seventeenth-Century England* (New York, 1969), notably chapter one. For Parker, see *Reproof*, p.227.

14.   *A Greek in the Temple* (1641), p.3. On religion at Cambridge see Fuller, *History of Cambridge University* (1655), pp.166–7, and J.B. Mullinger, *Cambridge Characteristics in the Seventeenth Century* (1867). For the Cambridge Platonists in particular, see the selection of their work edited by C.A. Patrides (1969).

15.   See N. Pevsner, *Cambridgeshire* (The Buildings of England series) (1954), p.110, and p.23ff. for the various and exciting building projects that were undertaken during Marvell's years at university—surely a neglected part of his visual education. On Peterhouse see A. Pritchard, 'Puritan Charges against Crashaw and Beaumont', *Times Literary Supplement*, 2 July 1964.

16.   Elsie Duncan-Jones, *A Great Master of Words. Some Aspects of Marvell's Poems of Praise and Blame* (The British Academy, London, 1976), p.3.

17.   Legouis, *André Marvell*, p.13.

18.   See L.N. Wall, 'Marvell and the Skinners', *Notes and Queries* (June 1962), p.219.

19.   Legouis, *Andrew Marvell*, p.9; *André Marvell*, p.20.

20.   'A Second Defence of the English People', *Complete Prose Works*, ed. D.M. Wolfe (Yale University Press), IV (1966), p.553; also in Columbia University Press edition of *The Works* VIII (1933), p.11. The work is praised by Marvell in a letter to Milton [II.305–6]. The following sentence (on good and bad systems) is cited by Augustine Birrell, *Andrew Marvell* (1905), p.23, as being the 'belief of a contemporary'.

21.   Peacham, *The Complete Gentleman* (1634), chapter xviii, 'Of Travaile'. The following quotation is from Halifax's *Complete Works*, ed. J.P. Kenyon (1969), p.96.

22.   See *T.L.S.* for 5 June 1924 and *Notes and Queries*, CCVII (1962), p.219.

23.   The best single study of the subject is J.W. Stoye, *English Travellers Abroad 1604–1667* (1952). I have also drawn upon *The Diary of John Evelyn*, ed. E.S. de

Beer (Oxford, 1955), the second volume of which contains an appendix on Evelyn's sources for his travel information; all references in the text are to this volume's foreign travel entries. Also useful have been *The Travels of Peter Mundy* (1924), William Brereton, *Travels in Holland*, etc. (1844) and Edward Browne, *An Account of Several Travels* (1677). See also, for Italian travel, note 30 below. Both Evelyn (May 1641) and Mundy (March 1640) left England at roughly the same time as Marvell; for their obtaining passes (exit permits) see Evelyn, p.29 and Mundy, IV.53.

24. *Instructions*, etc. (first edition 1642). All references are to that of 1650, here to p.5. For Milton's account of his travels see *Selected Prose*, ed. C.A. Patrides (1975), pp.67–70.

25. The remark by Montague is quoted in M.–S. Røstvig, *The Happy Man: Studies in the Metamorphosis of a Classical Ideal*, 2nd ed., 2 vols. (Oslo and New York, 1962, 1971), I.81. On Hawkins and the image of the *hortus conclusus* see Stanley Stewart, *The Enclosed Garden. The Tradition and the Image in Seventeenth-Century Poetry* (Madison, Milwaukee and London, 1966). For the Vaughan lines, see *The Works*, ed. L.C. Martin, 2nd ed. (1957), p.406, my italics.

26. This painting (once in the possession of William Morris) is based upon a 1565 drawing by the older Brueghel, now in the Albertina, Vienna; but such small gardens would have changed little in the intervening years. Pictures by the younger Brueghel are specifically noticed by Evelyn (p.70) at Brussels, along with others by Rubens and Titian.

27. See note in I.260–1 and, more generally, Rosalie Colie, *'My Ecchoing Song': Andrew Marvell's Poetry of Criticism* (Princeton, 1970), Donald M. Friedman, *Marvell's Pastoral Art* (1970), and Leishman's study, cited in note 38.

28. Stoye, op. cit., p.413.

29. On the virtuosi see 'The English Virtuoso in the Seventeenth Century', *Journal of the History of Ideas*, III (1942) pp.51–73 and 190–219. On their gardens it is worth consulting the essay on the Mollet family in *The French Formal Garden*, ed. E.B. MacDougall and F.H. Hazlehurst (Washington, D.C., 1974).

30. On Italian travel see A. Lytton Sells, *The Paradise of Travellers* (1964), Carlo Segré, *Itinerari di Stranieri in Italia* (Milan, 1938), Ludwig Schudt, *Italienreisen im 17 und 18 Jahrhundert* (Vienna-Munich, 1959), and George B. Parks, 'Travel as Education', in Richard Foster Jones *et al.*, *The Seventeenth Century* (Stanford, California, 1951). On Italian garden arts see, to start with, Georgina Masson, *Italian Gardens* (1961) and *The Italian Garden*, ed. David R. Coffin (Washington, D.C., 1972).

31. Printed in *The Harleian Miscellany*, XII (octavo ed. 1811). This tour was undertaken about 1610 and is useful for early attention to gardens, especially since its author showed some initiative, not frequently followed even by the end of the century, in going to such out-of-the-way places as the Villa Farnese at Caprarola (p.93).

32. *Crudities* (Glasgow, 1905; originally published 1611), I.292. References in the following pages to other travellers are as follows: Sandys, *A Relation of a Journey Begun An. Dom. 1610* 3rd ed. (1632); Raymond, *Il Mercurio Italico. An Itinerary containing a Voyage made through Italy in the year 1646, and 1647* (1648); Addison, *Works* (1721), volume II for 'Remarks on Several Parts of Italy', from which the Preface (no pagination) is quoted.

33. Marjorie H. Nicolson, 'Milton's Hell and the Phlegraean Fields', *University of Toronto Quarterly*, VII (1937), pp.500–13. For a rival claim see Irwin R. Blacker, 'Did Milton Visit Hell?', *Seventeenth-Century News*, IX (1951), p.54.

34. Sandys, *A Relation*, p.272. This fascination with the delightful confusions of art and nature is a constant theme in travellers' accounts of Italianate gardens; it is, of course, a central motif in Marvell's garden poems.

35. See Hans Henrik Brummer, *The Statue Court in the Vatican Belvedere* (Stockholm, 1970) and James S. Ackerman, 'The Belvedere as a Classical Villa', *Journal of the Warburg and Courtauld Institutes*, XIV (1951), pp.70–91.

36. On Milton in Italy see the life by W.R. Parker, 2 vols. (Oxford, 1968), John Arthos, *Milton and the Italian Cities* (1968) and the forthcoming study of Milton and art by Roland Mushat Frye (Princeton, 1978). Besides the epigrams to Leonora Baroni, Milton paid handsome tribute to Cardinal Barberini (in a letter to Lucan van Holste: Columbia edition of *Works*, XII.38–45).

37. Willughby's account is printed in John Ray, *Observations, Topographical, Moral and Physiological Made in a Journey*. . .(1673), pp.466–99. Peacham's remarks on Spain are on p.243 ff. of the work cited in note 21.

38. A useful collection of Cavalier poetry, from which (unless otherwise stated) all my examples are drawn, is *The Cavalier Poets*, ed. Robin Skelton (1970). I am also indebted to J.B. Leishman's *The Art of Marvell's Poetry* (1966), of which there is a fine, brief 'trailer' in his 1961 Warton Lecture at the British Academy, 'Some Themes and Variations in the Poetry of Andrew Marvell'.

39. See Bateson's note to E.B. Greenwood's 'Marvell's Impossible Love', *Essays in Criticism*, XXVII (1977), pp.110–11.

40. *Elements of Architecture* (1624), p.5. On Vasari's Studiolo see Luciano Berti, *Il Principe dello Studiolo. Francesco I dei Medici e la Fine del Rinascimento fiorentino* (Florence, 1967).

41. See *T.L.S.*, 8 August 1952 and, for other settings of Marvell's poems, I.247–8. Since William Lawes was killed, fighting for the Royalists, in September 1645, we may confidently place the poem's first composition before that date.

42. *A Greek in the Temple*, p.6.

43. The bibliography, of course, is huge. But start maybe with C.V. Wedgwood, *Oliver Cromwell* (revised and augmented edition, 1973), Christopher Hill, *God's Englishman: Oliver Cromwell and the English Revolution* (1970) and Maurice Ashley, *Oliver Cromwell and his world* (1972), all of which include suggestions for further reading, including more works by those three authors. A collection of essays, *The Interregnum: the Quest for a Settlement 1646–1660*, ed. G.E. Aylmer (1972) is also most valuable.

44. On the Latin sources and formal debts of the 'Ode' see especially A.J.N. Wilson's article in *The Critical Quarterly*, XI (1969), Rosemary Syfret's in *Review of English Studies*, n.s. XII (1961), and John Coolidge's in *Modern Philology*, LXIII (1965). Otherwise, there is a gathering of representative essays on the 'Ode' in the Penguin critical anthology, *Andrew Marvell*, ed. John Carey (1969), where the beginnings of a debate on the historical or critical readings of the poem between Douglas Bush and Cleanth Brooks can be found.

45. On the Banqueting House, still of course in existence, see Per Palme, *Triumph of Peace: A Study of the Whitehall Banqueting House* (1957) or the useful booklet by John Charlton (HMSO, 1964). On the masque generally see Stephen

Orgel, *The Illusion of Power: Political Theater in the English Renaissance* (Berkeley, 1975); for *Salmacida Spolia*, either Stephen Orgel and Roy Strong, *Inigo Jones, The Theatre of the Stuart Court*, 2 vols. (London and Berkeley, 1973), II.728 ff. or *A Book of Masques. In Honour of Allardyce Nicoll* (Cambridge, 1967), p.337 ff. The remark by James I, quoted later, is taken from Orgel and Strong, I.50.

46. Letter from John Newman, *T.L.S.*, 28 January 1972, part of a correspondence from 26 November 1971 to 11 February and 31 March 1972. One of the correspondents, James Turner, has kindly let me see his completed Oxford D.Phil. dissertation on topographical poetry between 1640 and 1660, but unfortunately too late to make use of in my text; when published it will add decisively to our reading of 'Upon Appleton House'. A recently published volume, *The Country House in English Renaissance Poetry* by W.A. McClung (Berkeley and Los Angeles, 1977) has nothing to contribute on Marvell and even perpetuates mistakes about the house at Nun Appleton.

47. Quotations from Fairfax's poetry are from the edition by E.B. Reed, in *Transactions of the Connecticut Academy of Arts and Sciences*, XIV (New Haven, 1909). An explanation, of course, of similarities in poems by Fairfax and Marvell is their debt to a common source, Saint-Amant (for details see notes to the poem in I.279 ff.). Apart from the poems which refer specifically to Fairfax localities, it is uncertain when other poems on nature and gardens (including the 'Mower' poems) were written; however, I consider them in this section, since we may surely assume that his stay at Nun Appleton gave Marvell some incentive for them. Two works are especially useful on this group of poems: that by Colie (see note 27) and Kitty Scoular, *Natural Magic* (Oxford, 1965).

48. *Pliny Letters*, 2 vols. (Loeb Classical Library, 1915), I.390 (for topiary reference) and I.154–8 (for winds, mentioned later).

49. See, for instance, Edmund Warcupp at Tivoli in *Italy in Its Originall Glory, Ruine and Revivall* (1660), pp.309–11, or Richard Lassels at Frascati in *The Voyage of Italy* (1670), pp.307–14. For a modern discussion of how gardens were designed to promote such meditations see David R. Coffin, *The Villa D'Este at Tivoli* (Princeton, 1960), where one of the most frequently visited of Italian gardens is the subject of a fascinating and learned study.

50. See *T.L.S.*, 11 November 1955, resumed as a note in I.284–5.

51. See especially the essay by Elizabeth MacDougall in *The Italian Garden* (above, note 30) for full discussion and other illustrations.

52. See Leishman's Warton Lecture (above, note 38), p.239 and notes at I.291.

53. Lassels, op. cit., p.208. Warcupp also (above, note 49) invokes masque imagery to narrate his visit to parts of the Villa D'Este. For further information on masques see material cited in note 45; it is by now a commonplace of Marvell criticism to note this theatrical imagery. For the Vitruvian shutters, see *De Architectura* (Loeb ed., 1931), I.288. On the aquatic displays in Florence see Roy Strong, *Splendour at Court* (1973), chapter 5 and plate 142.

54. King's treatise was first mentioned in this context by Kitty Scoular. On analogies with paintings in the Nun Appleton poem see Colie (above, note 27) and Mario Praz, *Modern Language Review*, XXI (1926), p.322.

55. D.C. Allen, *Image and Meaning* (1968), pp.205–12. On the oak and Charles I, later in the same paragraph, see Kitty Scoular, p.142, though, as Mrs Duncan-Jones has pointed out to me, the allusion to Charles I is highly unlikely, it

being a most uncomfortable subject in the Fairfax household. (But see also note 97).

56.   This is simply my own guess, to add to the obscurities of these years. But that no mention is recorded of an event that might well have eliminated Marvell from consideration for the post is surely no more improbable than that strange rumour we have of Marvell's collaboration with Milton in writing *Eikonoclastes*, hardly consistent with his writing of the 'Horatian Ode' (see Legouis, *André Marvell*, p.177 and note).

57.   Discussed by Frank Kermode in his introduction to the Arden edition of *The Tempest* and by myself in *A Critical Commentary on Shakespeare's 'The Tempest'* (1968).

58.   The point is made by Wallace, p.107. 'A Dialogue between Soul and Body' has resemblances to a work by James Howell of 1651-2 (see I.249). I have discussed 'A Dialogue, Between the Resolved Soul' etc. in this context largely for convenience; its possible allusions to *Paradise Lost* (see Marvell I.242) argue modestly for his having seen Milton's poem in manuscript at this stage of their friendship.

59.   The point is made by Birrell (above, note 20), p.63.

60.   *Andrew Marvell*, p.99. On the poem's being shown to the Queen of Sweden see *André Marvell*, p.189 note 68.

61.   On details of publication see notes at I.320. For some attempts to read the poem as a successful whole see Wallace, chapter 3, and the articles by James F. Carens, 'Andrew Marvell's Cromwell Poems', *Bucknell Review*, VII (1957), pp.41-70, and by J.A. Mazzeo, 'Cromwell as Davidic King' in *Reason and Imagination* (1962), pp.29-55.

62.   See Rudolf Wittkower, *Architectural Principles in the Age Of Humanism* (1949), Pt.IV.

63.   Sonnet 124. See on this theme the essay by L.C. Knights, 'Time's Subjects', in *Some Shakespearean Themes* (1960).

64.   '"Tom May's Death" and Ben Jonson's Ghost: A Study of Marvell's Satiric Method', *M.L.R.*, LXXI (1976), p.31. Like Mrs Rees, I accept Marvell's authorship of this satire; but for the alternative argument see *Andrew Marvell: Complete Poetry*, ed. George de F. Lord (New York, 1968), p.xxxii.

65.   By M.C. Bradbrook and M.G. Lloyd Thomas (above, note 2), p.78. On Marvell's being won over to the new regime, see Legouis, *Andrew Marvell*, p.92.

66.   This material was discovered by Elsie Duncan-Jones and communicated in letters to the *T.L.S.*, 2 December 1949, 31 July 1953 and 20 June 1958. See also Legouis, 'Marvell and "the two learned brothers of St. Marthe"', *Philological Quarterly*, XXXVIII (1959), pp.450-8.

67.   See *T.L.S.*, 20 June 1958 and Legouis, *André Marvell*, pp.199-201, for details of Marvell's employment and of when Meadows, preferred for the post in 1653, came to leave it. See also II.306 and 379-81 for an example of Marvell's letters while employed there.

68.   *The Poems of Edmund Waller*, ed. G. Thorn Drury (The Muses' Library, 1905), II.34-5, and *Poems and Fables of Dryden* (ed. cit.), pp.6-12. See also W. Arthur Turner, 'Milton, Marvell and "Dradon" at Cromwell's Funeral', *Philological Quarterly*, XXVIII (1949), pp.320-3.

69.   On Marvell's parliamentary career there are materials in Legouis, 'Andrew

Marvell: Further Biographical Points', *M.L.R.*, XVIII (1923), pp.418–26, and in those items cited in note 79.

70. Legouis, *Andrew Marvell*, p.129; for his scuffle in the House, see the article cited in note 69.

71. Suggested by Bradbrook and Thomas, p.6. See also their appendix C for a possible contact between Marvell and the young Spinoza during this visit to Holland.

72. Guy Miège, *A Relation of Three Embassies...* (1669), p.5; all further quotations in this section are from this work, except those from Carlisle's letters, for which see Caroline Robbins, 'Carlisle and Marvell in Russia, Sweden and Denmark 1663–1664', *The History of Ideas News Letter*, III/i (1957), pp.8–17; quotations from these letters from Carlisle in Marvell's hand are not specially noted. Miège's account of the Russian part of the trip was re-issued in 1926 as a school text, called *A Journey to Russia*, and some extracts are also reprinted in Bradbrook and Thomas, appendix B. As Legouis notes (*Andrew Marvell*, p.131), Marvell might have read Milton's *A Brief History of Moscovia*, a compilation of travellers' tales, written before 1650, not published till 1682. Milton's *History* is printed in the Columbia *Works*, X.327–82.

73. *Andrew Marvell*, p.133; on Marvell's receiving the sturgeon's head see *André Marvell*, p.252 and notes.

74. I use George de F. Lord's excellent *Anthology of Poems on Affairs of State* (New Haven, 1975), from which all quotations in this section are taken and to the commentary in which I am much indebted; the poem quoted in this paragraph is from p.43. For discussions of the authenticity of these poems see George de F. Lord, 'Two New Poems by Marvell?', *Bulletin of the New York Public Library*, LXII (1958), pp.551–70 and succeeding discussions by Lord and Ephim G. Fogel in the same *Bulletin*, LXIII (1959), pp.223–36, 292–308 and 355–66.

75. See M.T. Osborne's *Advice-to-a-Painter Poems 1633–1856* (Austin, Texas, 1949) and David Cordingly, *Marine Painting in Britain 1700–1900* (1974).

76. *The Diary of Samuel Pepys*, ed. R. Latham and W. Matthews (1970 *et seq.*), VIII.21.

77. Quotations from 'Last Instructions' continue to be from Lord's *Anthology*. I'm indebted to Wallace's chapter for details in my own discussion of this poem; see also Earl Miner, 'The "Poetic Picture, Painted Poetry" of *The Last Instructions to a Painter*', *Modern Philology*, LXIII (1966), pp.288–94, and A.S. Fisher, 'The Augustan Marvell: *The Last Instructions to a Painter*', *English Literary History*, XXXVIII (1971), pp.223–38, and Michael Gearin-Tosh, 'The Structure of Marvell's "Last Instructions to a Painter"', *Essays in Criticism*, XX (1972), pp.48–57.

78. See notes 69 and 70. The Speaker, Sir Edward Turner, who ruled against Marvell on that occasion, also gets his come-uppance: lines 863–84.

79. Wallace, p.179. Milward's diary (next paragraph) has been edited by Caroline Robbins (Cambridge, 1938); see especially p.lxxv. See also her note on another of Marvell's speeches, *M.L.R.*, XXXI (1936), pp.549–50, from which I quote later.

80. *History of My Own Times*, ed. O. Airy, 3 vols. (Oxford, 1897–1902), I.467–8.

81. *The Diary of Samuel Pepys*, VII.416. See also John S. Coolidge, 'Martin Marprelate, Marvell and *Decorum Personae* as a Satirical Theme', *Proceedings of the*

Modern Language Association, 74 (1959), pp.526–32.

82. Legouis, *Andrew Marvell*, p.145 and *André Marvell*, pp.273–4.

83. Swift's debt to Marvell is discussed by Irvin Ehrenpreis, *Modern Language Notes*, LXX (1955) and by Ronald Paulson, *Theme and Structure in Swift's Tale of a Tub* (1960), notably pp.39–45 and 238–45. There also seem to me moments in *The Rehearsal Transpros'd* when Marvell anticipates Sterne's manoeuvres in *Tristram Shandy*: for example, p.39, line 30, p.85, lines 10–13, p.121.

84. *Andrew Marvell*, p.104.

85. Marvell's nephew, Popple, was to translate the Latin of John Locke's *Treatise on Tolerance* in 1689, so these convictions evidently ran in the family. See also W.K. Jordan, *The Development of Religious Toleration in England*, 3 vols. (1932–7).

86. Parker's was *A Reproof to the Rehearsal Transpros'd*; the others were *Rosemary and Bayes, A Common-place-book out of the Rehearsal Transpros'd, The transproser rehearsed, S'too him Bayes* and the work by Hickeringill (note 6).

87. Legouis, *Andrew Marvell*, p.146, and Wallace, p.204 respectively; see latter's whole chapter (5) on these prose controversies.

88. Texts of this 'Mock Speech' may be found in Bradbrook and Thomas, pp.125–7 (the version from which I quote) and in *Andrew Marvell Selected Poetry and Prose*, ed. Dennis Davison (1952).

89. Grey's *Debates*, IV.328–31.

90. Legouis, *Andrew Marvell*, pp.161–2. For a full account of Marvell's last years, including his 'marriage' and death, see F.S. Tupper, 'Mary Palmer, alias Mrs Andrew Marvell', *P.M.L.A.*, LIII (1938), pp.367–90; a summary of Tupper's intricate article constitutes appendix A in Bradbrook and Thomas. See also the Marvell entry in *Dictionary of National Biography*.

91. Respectively Thompson, ed. cit., III.491 and Grosart, I.lii note.

92. The first version was told by Marvell's editor, Thomas Cooke, in 1726 and is reprinted in the modern edition, I.403. The second version, drawn apparently from an Irish pamphlet of 1754, was recounted by Captain Thompson in 1776 and is reprinted in Grosart, I.xlix.

93. *Calendar*, p.496 (reprinted Legouis, *André Marvell*, p.271) for the Colonel Blood incident. For the hints of his spying see K.H.D. Haley, *William of Orange and the English Opposition, 1672–4* (Oxford, 1953), pp.57–9.

94. The references in this paragraph are drawn from Legouis. The claim for Marvell as England's 'Centinel' is from an anonymous poem, 'On his Excellent Friend, Mr Andrew Marvell', *Poems on affairs of State* (5th ed., 1703), I.122–3. Swift's pleasure is recorded in *A Tale of a Tub*, ed. Herbert Davis (Oxford, 1965), p.5. For the Lamb references see 'The Old Benchers of the Inner Temple', *Essays of Elia* (1823) and 'Blakesmoor in H——shire', *Last Essays of Elia* (1833). Wordsworth, the sonnet 'Great men have been among us' and *Early Letters of William and Dorothy Wordsworth*, ed. Selincourt (1935), p.541.

95. Wallace, p.206; *The Latin Poetry*, ed. cit., p.4.

96. *Latin Poetry*, p.6. But what then of his Highgate retreat, in those days still a country village, as Charles Cotton versified it: 'being pass'd through High-gate there/I was saluted by the Countrey Air'?

97. See above at various points of my discussion pp.65, 130, 131 and 164. It also seems to me totally consistent with what I have tried throughout to show of Marvell's character (notably his appetite for many perspectives—see pp.129–30, his sense of

conviction and commitment yet his acute sense of self-protection) that he would return to poems and revise them in the light of later events, later changes in his opinions, whether political or poetical. It seems possible, for example, that the critics who read an allusion to Charles I into 'Upon Appleton House', stanza LXX, may be dealing with a later reworking of the poem once Marvell had left the Fairfax household in which such a reference would not have been appropriate in a piece actually addressed 'to my Lord Fairfax'. On possible revisions see I.315 among other examples and I.253 (may not the dating of the allusion to the Jews' conversion be the poet's playfulness with his own return to an earlier poem?).

98.   Quoted Bradbrook and Thomas, pp.140–1 from B.M. Add. MS 8,888.

Postscript: When this book was in the final stages of printing the discovery was announced of a portrait miniature of Marvell (plate 66, p.190). It was found in the Texas Humanities Research Center at Austin by Professor Norman K. Farmer Jr, who will be writing about his discovery in a forthcoming issue of *English Literary Renaissance*. The miniature may well be that by Cooper discussed above (see p.16 and note 8).

Chronology

1621	31 March. Andrew Marvell born at Winestead-in-Holderness, Yorkshire, son of clergyman
1624	Marvell family moves to neighbouring Hull when father is appointed Lecturer at Holy Trinity Church. Andrew Marvell educated at Hull Grammar School
1633	Enters Trinity College, Cambridge
1637	Publishes first verses in a university volume of congratulatory poems on birth of a daughter to King Charles and Queen Henrietta Maria
1638	Mother dies (April), father remarries (November)
1641	Father dies and Marvell leaves Cambridge
1640s	Spends four years abroad, visiting Holland, France, Italy and Spain. Has returned home by
1648	(February) writes poem 'To his Noble Friend Mr Richard Lovelace' and later that year and in 1649 other Royalist verses
1649	King Charles executed
1650	Cromwell returns from Ireland; some time thereafter Marvell writes 'An Horatian Ode'
1650s	Early years of decade is living in Yorkshire as tutor to Mary Fairfax at Nun Appleton
1653	Back in London; in touch with Milton; appointed tutor to William Dutton, later Cromwell's ward, and lives with him at Eton
1655	'The First Anniversary of the Government under his Highness the Lord Protector' written
1656	In France with his pupil, Dutton
1657	Appointed Latin Secretary to the Council of State
1658	Writes poem on the death of Oliver Cromwell
1659	Elected Member of Parliament for Hull—a position held till his death
1662–3	In Holland for eleven months
1663–5	Secretary to the embassy of the Earl of Carlisle to Russia, Sweden and Denmark
1665	(January) returns to England
1667	'The Last Instructions to a Painter' written
1672	His prose satire against Archdeacon Parker, *The Rehearsal Transpros'd*, published anonymously
1673	Writes and publishes second part of *The Rehearsal Transpros'd* under his name
1674	Writes commendatory verses for *Paradise Lost* (2nd ed.)
1676	Publishes further prose work, *Mr Smirk: Or the Divine in Mode* under assumed name
1677	Further prose, *An Account of the Growth of Popery and Arbitrary Government*, published anonymously
1678	16 August dies of a tertian ague
1681	*Miscellaneous Poems* published by his 'widow', Mary Marvell

Index

Index

Index